A Message of Hope
from the Angels

Also by Lorna Byrne

Angels in my Hair
Stairways to Heaven

From the time that Lorna Byrne was born in Ireland in 1953, she has been seeing and communicating with angels. She sees them physically, as clearly as the rest of us see someone standing in front of us.

Lorna has continued seeing and talking with angels throughout her life and says 'They were my teachers, my friends, and they still are today.' When she was growing up, Lorna was told by the angels not to tell anyone what she saw. She didn't until she wrote the book *Angels in my Hair* in 2008.

Angels in my Hair is now an international bestseller, translated into twenty-four languages and published in more than fifty countries. Lorna's second book, *Stairways to Heaven*, is also an international bestseller. *A Message of Hope from the Angels* is Lorna's third book.

The overwhelming response of readers to Lorna's message – regardless of religious beliefs – is that she gives them back hope, helping them to realise that no matter how alone they might feel they have a guardian angel by their side.

Lorna is a widow with four children and lives quietly in rural Ireland

For more information, please visit www.lornabyrne.com

Lorna Byrne

A Message of Hope
from the Angels

CORONET

First published in Great Britain in 2012 by Coronet
An imprint of Hodder & Stoughton
An Hachette UK company

1

A CIP catalogue record for this title is available from the British Library

ISBN 978 1 444 72987 0

Typeset in Sabon MT by Palimpsest Book Production Limited,
Falkirk, Stirlingshire

Printed and bound by
Clays Ltd, St Ives plc, Bungay, Suffolk

Hodder & Stoughton policy is to use papers that are natural, renewable
and recyclable products and made from wood grown in sustainable forests.
The logging and manufacturing processes are expected to conform to the
environmental regulations of the country of origin.

Hodder & Stoughton Ltd
338 Euston Road
London NW1 3BH

www.hodder.co.uk

To the growth of peace within us all and throughout the world.

Contents

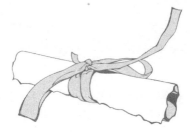

CHAPTER ONE

A message of hope for these challenging times

'THE ANGEL OF HOPE IS A BEACON OF LIGHT IN all our lives. He helps to keep the light of hope burning inside all of us throughout our lives,' the angel told me. 'Hope plays an enormous part in everyone's life. Hope makes the impossible possible.'

I was about twelve years old when an angel told me this.

I have been seeing and talking with angels since I was a little baby. I see angels every day and I see them physically as I see someone sitting in front of me. Angels are my friends and companions and I talk with them all the time, sometimes using words and sometimes without words. I have no idea why I should be able to see angels and you don't. I'm just an ordinary person.

I had seen the Angel of Hope previously, but this day when I was twelve was the first time that I learnt who this particular angel was and how he helps us.

The Angel of Hope doesn't look like any other angel I have ever seen. He looks like a massive flame. Within this very bright flame I am shown a faint human appearance, which is masculine, and a beautiful dazzling emerald green colour, holding a torch – like an Olympic flame. The brightness of the Angel of Hope looks different to any other angel; I think this is because it's a light within a light.

The Angel of Hope is enormous, the height of a mature tree. When I see him he always seems to be very far away from me. So he should then look small, but he's always massive. It's quite strange – it's as if he's very far away but right in front of me at the same time, hard as that is to explain.

He seems to be forever moving, turning back constantly to encourage whoever he is leading at the time with a gentle smile. His expression is one of love and encouragement.

Lately I have been seeing the Angel of Hope a lot

more than I would have previously. I probably see him every day. People seem to be needing hope so much at this time.

All those years ago, the angel showed me a vision of the Angel of Hope at work, so that I could understand more about him. I was shown the Angel of Hope guiding soldiers through a trench battlefield. I have no idea what nationality the soldiers were. I was shown one particular soldier crawling exhausted through the mud. I could see he was injured. The Angel of Hope was moving in front of him, constantly beckoning him forward. I was allowed to see through the soldier's eyes. The soldier could not see the Angel of Hope, but he saw a light and within this light the soldier could see those he loved – his wife and young children, his elderly parents. The Angel of Hope was giving him the strength to stay alive, encouraging him not to give up, by giving him hope of a reunion with the family he loved.

'Do you understand, Lorna?' the angel said. 'The Angel of Hope can't stop the war, heal this soldier or rescue him, but he can give him the strength to make it to where he can be rescued.' The angel smiled at me and continued. 'That soldier died in his bed many years later.' I was so pleased with this news. The love that the young soldier had for his family was very beautiful.

Whenever things have been difficult for me and my family I see the Angel of Hope there, trying to give me encouragement. This is in addition to my guardian angel and the other angels who will be around me helping.

I remember one particular period – being very stressed and worried about whether my husband Joe would get a job. He had been sick for a long time and off work but was now well enough to work. This was the 1980s in Ireland though: things were tough and jobs were hard to find. We had three children to feed and I used to worry desperately. I kept on seeing the Angel of Hope, in the distance, turning towards me and smiling in encouragement. He kept the hope burning inside of me that Joe would eventually be successful in getting one of the jobs that he had applied for. It was quite a while before he did, and I was almost despairing – but not quite. Seeing the Angel of Hope kept me going throughout this difficult period and helped me in giving encouragement and support to Joe. Joe was eventually successful in finding employment.

The importance of hope should never be under-estimated. With hope in our heart we can do so much.

I know a family whose second child was born with severe genetic difficulties. The doctors had told the parents that there was only a small chance their little girl would walk. The first time I saw this child she was about nine months old. As her parents chatted to me with her in her father's arms they were surrounded by angels who were very tall, a bright translucent white and gave a female appearance. I could vaguely see wings. As with all angels, they were extremely beautiful. One of the angels told me, without words, that this family would not give up hope that this child would walk, no matter what the doctors said. As we talked, the father put the baby on the floor and the angels around her encouraged her to move her legs and kick.

The Angel of Hope appeared for one moment. His light was so bright and it was as if everything disappeared except for the parents and the child. It was as if the parents could see the light of the Angel of Hope and could see his encouraging smile and were being filled with the light of hope. I know that every time they encountered a problem in relation to their daughter, the Angel of Hope would instil in them the courage to keep going.

The Angel of Hope is one angel, but he is there to help everyone and can be in many places at once. In this he is like an archangel. He is there, briefly, whenever people need hope to lead them on and give them courage. Of course, other angels help to give us hope too.

I see a guardian angel with everyone, regardless of their religion or nationality. I have never seen anyone, anywhere in the world, without a guardian angel. Your guardian angel is with you from before you are conceived until after your death and never leaves you even for one moment. It loves you unconditionally and will do everything possible to guide you through life and keep you filled with hope. Your guardian angel can let other angels in to help you too.

A year or so later I saw the child again. There were lots of adults there and the child was being passed from one to another, the focus of everyone's love and attention. The child looked so bright to me, and the angels told me it was because of the level of encouragement the whole family was giving to the child. They were clearly all listening to their guardian angels and playing their part. At one stage, the father put the little one standing beside him. It was beautiful to see the angels encircling the child to try and keep her wobbly little legs strong, to stop them from giving under her. She is now three and she is walking. Not only is she walking but they had brought her to the beach recently and she had started to run – if not very steadily.

The parents and all of the family kept the light of

hope burning for this child. They helped her to walk and are now hoping she will learn to talk properly too. This child is a beacon of hope and the light of this hope has lit up the family, filling them and giving them hope in other areas of their lives. And it's not just the immediate family – the wider family and neighbours have been inspired and filled with hope as a result of this example.

> **I see a lot of angels holding lights in front of people, helping to encourage them.**

I see angels all of the time working hard to give us hope. I was sitting in a hotel reception recently, waiting for a journalist to arrive. The angels with me told me to get up and go and sit in the lounge. There was a man sitting at a low table by the window. On the table in front of him were some papers and a laptop. There were four angels sitting surrounding him. One of the angels was holding a bright light, about the size of a marble, in front of the man at chest height. When I see an angel holding a light in front of someone, I know that the person is having a tough time and that the angel is holding the light to help to give them hope and the courage to keep on going.

One of the angels told me without words that the man was extremely worried and stressed over his business. I have no idea what his business was. The angels were encouraging him to see a solution and they told me there was a solution somewhere within the papers, but he was too anxious to see it. One of the angels was trying to calm him down while one of the others kept reaching out and pointing to one particular sheet of paper. When he did this, the man would reach out to the sheet of paper but didn't seem to be seeing the solution. All of the time he was writing notes and crossing things out on his writing pad. At times, the light would get brighter for a moment and, without the angels telling me, I knew that was him seeing a glimpse of a solution, a glimpse of hope, a way out of his business difficulties. I sat there for about twenty minutes, as the journalist was late. I prayed for the businessman to find the solution. My heart went out to him. He looked so stressed and concerned. As I left, I asked the four angels around the table if he would see the solution before the day was out, and I was told that he mightn't see the whole solution but that he would at least have the idea and over the next few days he would find a solution to the problem.

These days I see a lot of angels holding lights in front of people, helping to encourage them. I see angels helping to kindle hope in us all the time – hope at an individual, a community, a national or a global level.

Hope often starts with the little initiatives. One evening a few weeks ago, I came across a group of neighbours cleaning up a green near where I live. It's an area which has looked grubby and neglected for a long time. As they worked they were surrounded by angels, who were whispering in their ears, encouraging them. As I walked past one the angel said to me, 'Can you see the hope that is stirred up in these people?' I smiled and the angel continued: 'Through small steps like this they can make their world a better place.'

The following day, I walked past the green again. I was amazed at how different it was. They had picked up the litter, cut the grass and tidied up the flowerbed. The entire place felt so much brighter. One of the angels who was there called my attention to a little blackbird that was able to find a worm in the soil they had loosened. I had seen no birds there the day before.

Hope brings a community together to make things better and when it does I see people get brighter, shine more and then they can go on to achieve greater things. People who believe things can be changed for the better are beacons of light for us – and need to be supported.

Hope can be given to others. It gives strength and courage and then hope grows. We all have a part to play in growing hope. In the past, people looked to leaders of churches, communities, businesses, countries to provide a vision of hope for the future, but now many of our leaders are struggling. They are failing to see the hope that is in front of them. They are failing to see all the ways in which we can make our world a better place to live.

The angels have told me so much about hope and how much we have to be hopeful about, and have showed me so many different ways in which they help to give us hope.

Everything I share with you in this book is from God and his angels. This book is a message of hope that has been given to me to share with each and every one of you, to help grow the light of hope within you.

CHAPTER TWO

You are loved
unconditionally

THE GUARDIAN ANGEL WITH THE LITTLE GIRL WAS
enormous. It towered over her and surrounded her
– like a half-circle curved around her, as she played
in the grassy area with her tiny black and white puppy.

I was walking through the grounds of Kilkenny
Castle when I saw her and as I kept walking I kept
watching. The angel did what I see many guardian
angels doing with children – as she sat there having
fun with her puppy it made itself smaller so it didn't
dwarf her.

The guardian angel didn't give an appearance of

being either male or female. It was bright and a golden amber colour. The clothes that were draped over it seemed to be made of enormous oval beads, which were amber in colour. Through the oval-shaped beads I could see the light reflecting – giving the angel an appearance of unusual depth.

This guardian angel's face looked extremely round and very translucent. I cannot describe the love that shone from this guardian angel's face as it looked down at the child. Its eyes were like crystal, yet full of life. A lot of the time, angels' eyes don't have a colour any more than the stars have a colour. But I could see a hint of that beautiful golden amber colour slightly shining from this angel's eyes. I smiled, looking at the beauty of this. The guardian angel smiled back at me, knowing what I was noticing.

The guardian angel knelt down beside the little girl and reached its hand out beside the child's hand to play with the puppy. The guardian angel's hands seemed to be bigger and more radiant than the rest of it. The hands were long and slender and yet enormous. They were translucent and were that same beautiful amber colour. The fingers of the hand seemed to stand out, so I could see light and movement inside them.

I watched the guardian angel's fingers of light

moving with such gentleness, love and care for the little girl and her puppy. I spoke to the angel without words, asking, 'Can she feel the presence of your hand?' The guardian angel replied as it stretched out its hand towards the little girl's hand again and touched it. 'Watch, Lorna.' The child burst out laughing with excitement and giggles and I knew straight away that the child did feel the touch of her guardian angel's hand.

I continued walking, moved by what I had seen. The little girl had Down's syndrome, and her guardian angel had been showing me how much she was loved, how well she was cared for. To angels we are all perfect – we humans see differences, and sometimes think one person is better than another, but to angels we are all perfect.

For the first few years of my life I saw a guardian angel standing behind everyone, but I found this very disorientating as guardian angels are brighter than any other angel. When I was about five, an angel told me that in future I would be shown guardian angels as a column of bright light behind a person. The guardian angel would only open up and show itself in what I call its full glory if there was some reason for it. I continue to see other angels physically and fully; it is only guardian angels that I am shown more often than not as a column of light.

When the light of a guardian angel opens up and I am shown the love of a guardian angel for the person it guards, I am so moved. So much love and compassion radiates from them. Regardless of how you behave, your guardian angel loves you unconditionally and will not judge you in any way. They won't find fault with you or criticise you. Your guardian angel will do everything within its power – without overstepping the boundary of your free will – to guide you and help to make life as easy as possible for you. Your guardian angel fills your life with the light of hope.

No one is unloved. If you feel that no loves and cares for you – you are wrong. Your guardian angel is there behind every moment of your life, and is pouring its love out on you continually.

I felt quite unloved as a child and a teenager. The doctors had told my parents when I was a baby that I was retarded, because I seemed to be more interested in what was going on around me – watching angels – than watching them. I know my parents loved me but they rarely showed it. I think they thought that I had no feelings. Feeling the love my guardian angel had for me, and the love of the other angels around me, was extremely important to me at this time.

Ask your guardian angel to allow you to feel its love – even a little of it. You can ask by talking to your guardian angel silently or aloud. I talk to my guardian angel as I do my friends.

Some people prefer to write their guardian angel a note or letter. If you do this, leave it somewhere for a few days – in a drawer or a place that feels appropriate to you – and then if it feels right you can burn it.

Whatever way you communicate with your guardian angel it will hear you.

If you keep asking, you will, over time, feel a joy stirring up inside of you and will start to feel better within yourself. It's as if your guardian angel, through allowing you to feel its love, allows your own self-love to grow. It takes time, though, and for most people this is not easy. It is up to you to recognise that love stirring inside of you, acknowledge it and say to yourself, 'I accept this gift.' The gift of love will grow more and more within you, and then you will start to share that love with others.

One of the most important things we all have to learn is how to love ourselves more. Instead of seeing all the imperfections within yourself you need to see the beauty within yourself. You need to learn to see yourself as your guardian angel sees you. You need to allow yourself to see the sweetness, the compassion, the love that is within you.

You may not think you are good enough, you may even use the word hopeless about yourself, but however you judge yourself your guardian angel is so proud of you.

Your guardian angel is there behind you every moment of your life.

I have often seen a guardian angel trying to help the self-love of the person it is guarding to grow. It is very beautiful to see. The guardian angel, who is, of course, so much bigger than the person it is guarding, bows over the person and slowly and gently brings its right arm in front of the person at heart level. With its hand open wide, the angel makes circular motions in front of the area of the heart; this can go on for several minutes, but sometimes lasts only a few seconds. One guardian angel I saw doing this to a young woman told me he was opening her up to love herself, helping her to experience good and positive feelings and thoughts about herself.

Your guardian angel will also call in the help of other guardian angels so the people they are minding will pay you compliments, or give you a pat on the back. This is why it is so important not to ignore compliments or presume they are false, and to thank the person who has paid you the compliment.

Your guardian angel will also try and stop people saying insulting or hurtful things to you, but as everyone has free will the angels don't always succeed.

If you don't love yourself, ask your guardian angel for help to love yourself as your guardian angel loves you.

I have met so many men, women and – sad to say – children who don't know how to love themselves or others. Millions of people around the world don't know how to love because they have never been taught to love. Children of today are learning how to express anger, impatience and jealousy – how to express emotions that help them to get their own way – but are not learning about love. It's as if many people have forgotten how to love. Love is inside each and every one of us but we have forgotten how to express it.

Children need to be shown that it's OK to love, and to be shown this both in the home and in the wider community. Children learn so much from example. The little gestures – like a gentle touch of the hand, an embrace from one parent to the other when they come home, the gift of a flower – are so important. These little expressions of love can be simple, and yet are so significant. Children are watching you carefully for signs of love and when they see them they too experience love. It nurtures and helps grow the love that dwells inside them.

We should never underestimate the transformative power of love. Love can change people so much and has the power to change the world we live in into a wonderful place. Children are our future, so is vital we teach our children to love both by showing them by example, and by talking about the importance of love. Children are everyone's responsibility not just their mother's and father's. As we all teach children how to love, we will all learn more about love and open more to love ourselves. Throughout our lives, regardless of our age, we have to be shown love. When we are shown love by anyone, even a stranger, it stirs up the love within us and makes it stronger, shining through us.

The potential for love is limitless; we are all capable of giving and receiving unlimited love. Loving one person does not mean you have less to give to another. No one is unlovable or undeserving of love, regardless of how you might judge their past actions, and no one is incapable of love.

Love stirs up compassion within our hearts and helps us to reach out and help each other. This precious gift of love dwells within each and every one of us and whether we realise it or not we yearn for love.

Ask your guardian angel to help open your eyes to start to see the expressions of love all around you – in your home, your workplace, on the street, in shops – anywhere and everywhere. Help children – and adults – around you to see these signs of love also.

I hug almost everyone I meet. I have met many people, men women and children who rarely have been hugged – not even as a child by their parents. Sometimes when I have hugged someone they don't know what to do and have held back, wondering if it's OK to be hugged. Sometimes I have to reassure them with words that it is safe. Then I slowly feel them embrace me. It's as if they are drinking in the love that I am giving them freely and they are feeling it for the first time in their life. I feel so sad when I feel this with anyone. It's so sad to think that they are so unaware of the precious gift of love that is within them.

I was in a hotel in Dublin one day; I had got there early for an interview and was sitting in a quiet corner sipping a glass of water. A woman came over to me and told me she had seen me talking about angels on the TV. She introduced herself as Stefanie and asked if she could talk with me for a few minutes. She was surrounded by angels and right behind her was the light of her guardian angel. There were four angels fussing around her, touching her hair, trying to give her comfort and keep her calm so she could talk to me. I didn't know at the time what the problem was, as they didn't say anything to me and her guardian angel didn't open up.

She sat down and started to talk straight away, telling me of her two teenage children, a boy of thirteen and a girl of fifteen. She told me her daughter had told her that she hated her and wished she was dead. Stefanie wept as she told me that her daughter regularly screamed at her, telling her she was no good, that she hadn't got a clue. She compared her mum to other mums, saying that hers was the ugliest mum in the world and that all her schoolfriends' mums were wonderful.

For two years her daughter had constantly been running Stefanie down, saying unbelievably horrible things. Stefanie was completely broken; she was shattered. Her daughter had stripped her of all her confidence and belief in herself both as a mother and as a person. It had reached a stage where Stefanie was so anxious and upset that she couldn't sleep, had to take time off work and had been prescribed medication for depression. Unfortunately, her husband was of little help or support. Stefanie also told me rather shamefacedly that she screamed and shouted back at her daughter, that she couldn't seem to control herself.

As Stefanie talked, the angels were talking to me, without words, as well. They told me I was to ask Stefanie an important question. I took a deep breath and did as they asked.

'When did you last tell your daughter that you loved her?'

Stefanie looked at me with astonishment, replying, 'She's my daughter. She knows I love her.'

I took Stefanie's hand and waited a little before replying, as the angels were telling me to.

'Are you sure she does? Think back to when your daughter was a child. How much love did you show her? How often did you take her in your arms and hug her tightly, telling her you loved her? Telling her how precious she was?'

Stefanie looked at me with a confused expression. 'My mother never did that. My mother never told me she loved me, but she was my mother – so I know she must have loved me.'

The angels were talking to me all the time as I replied, 'Your daughter is crying out for your love. Strange as it may seem, it is love that she is actually showing you but you don't recognise it. Who else could she say all those horrible things to? Who else could she tell all the frustrations and confusions she feels as a teenager?'

I continued. 'Try to stop reacting angrily to your daughter. I know it's really hard but try and not take it personally. Start to tell her and show her the love you have for her. You may think she doesn't hear your words, but she does. Your daughter needs you; the world is a frightening place at the moment for her and she just needs to know you're there for her and that you will never leave her.' I smiled at Stefanie. 'Show her your love in little ways.'

Stefanie looked at me with her eyes full of tears. 'But I don't think I know how to do this.'

'Ask your guardian angel to help you,' I replied. 'It will help to show you little things that count, the first steps that you both need to take. Later, you can take bigger steps. Start today to show your daughter love in small ways, to reach out to her. Has she a favourite thing she likes to eat, like cupcakes? Well, make them. Don't scream and shout, just talk from your heart. Love is so powerful it can transform all things — I know you're going to get such a surprise with the love you get back from your daughter. And remember also, your son is watching everything that is going on; he too needs to know that you love him.'

We said our goodbyes. I prayed a lot for Stefanie and her children for months – prayers that they would let love grow within the family

I rarely remember faces and a year or so later I was in a big department store in Dublin and a woman with a teenager came up to me and introduced herself. It was Stefanie and her daughter, whom she introduced to me as Sam. Sam was a beautiful, tall, dark-haired girl with a happy smile on her face. Stefanie told me that she had acted on what I had said that day, and had asked her guardian angel for help. She described what happened the first time she made the cupcakes Sam loved. She had been putting the icing on top when her daughter came into the kitchen. Her daughter took one and as she left the kitchen Stefanie just said, 'I love you.' There was no response from her daughter.

Sam stood beside her as she told me this and then interrupted, saying, 'I was a horrible person then. Then one day we were having a row and Mum again said that she loved me I burst into tears. I told Mum that day that I never knew she loved me.'

Sam smiled at me and then at Stefanie, saying, 'Mum, I love you.' It was just beautiful to see the compassion in her face as she said this. Stefanie put her arm around Sam and gave her a big hug, saying, 'I love you too.' I was so happy as they went on their way.

The precious gift of love is inside each and every one of us – and we all need to learn how to let this love grow so that we can reach out to others with compassion. It starts with the little things: a smile, a kind word, a hug. Inside each and every one of us is this unconditional love and, if we will allow it, it will fill our lives with hope and compassion.

People suppress love, and this lack of love can show in many ways. It may be in getting pleasure or enjoyment out of someone's hard luck; it may be in bad-mouthing someone or spreading gossip; it may be in being judgmental and critical or getting impatient and frustrated with those around you. You may not mean to do this; it may be a habit, or something that people around you do. Try and recognise this behaviour in yourself, try and recognise when you fail to show love and compassion so that you can learn for the next time.

Your guardian angel shows you unconditional love and if you ask it will help you to learn to love yourself and others more. You know that feeling of unease you have inside of you when you have been mean or unfair to someone? That's your guardian angel teaching you about love. Learn to recognise and acknowledge these feelings, even if it is uncomfortable to do so. It is only in responding to these nudges from our guardian angels that we all learn to love more.

Remember: you are unconditionally loved; ask your guardian angel to help you to feel its love, and to stir up the love that is inside of you. Ask your guardian angel to help you to see the abundance of love in people around you and to notice the expressions of this love.

CHAPTER THREE

Help is always close at hand

EVERY DAY, I SEE ANGELS HELPING PEOPLE DOING things. Things we assume we are doing on our own, when in fact an angel is there, helping.

Sometimes, on a sunny day, walking through the grounds of the university near where I live, I see students sitting on stone seats opposite the library or sitting on the grass studying and I see teacher angels with some of them.

Teacher angels always seem to be holding something – a symbol of learning that is relevant to whatever they are teaching. Sometimes they are holding a book or a pointer or a board with writing on it with the words constantly changing. I once saw a bricklayer's apprentice with a teacher angel who had a trowel in his hand. Teacher angels exhibit the mannerisms we associate with teachers.

I have often seen a teacher angel standing in front of a student, book in hand. The book would look similar to the one the student was working with and seem to be open at the same page. Occasionally I see the teacher angel turn to another page and I smile, knowing that the teacher angel is having difficulty with his student, who is finding it hard to make progress. I have seen teacher angels stretch out their hands and touch a student gently on the head with one finger, trying to get the student's attention. Most of the time this seems to work, but sometimes not. Teacher angels never give up, though, and never lose their patience. I have seen teacher angels blowing on a student's book and making the page turn, or causing a strong breeze, which blows some of the student's books and pens onto the ground. That is the teacher angel trying to bring the student's attention to a particular page or subject, or to simply stop them daydreaming. Teacher angels work very hard to get their students' attention.

I am always amazed at how few people have teacher angels. After all, all they have to do is ask their guardian angel for help with whatever they are learning and their guardian angel will invite a teacher angel in. In the college I know best only about one student in ten has a teacher angel with them. For some reason I don't understand, music students seem to ask the angels for help more. When I pass the area where they wait for their individual music classes I see more teacher angels – but there are still only teacher angels with about one in five of these music students. It seems such a shame, when God has given us teacher angels to help us, not to take up this opportunity. If you are learning anything – to cook, to play golf, to use a computer, to drive a car, to speak a language, to have patience with your child, to meditate – then ask your guardian angel to invite in a teacher angel to help. Don't worry about what sort of angel, or teacher angel, would be best: your guardian angel will know, so just ask them.

> **Never feel that you are not deserving of help. We are all deserving of help and the angels love to help us.**

The angels tell me that there is an unlimited number of teacher angels, and we should never hesitate to ask for help. Your asking for a teacher angel does not take an angel away from someone else. There is an abundance of teacher angels. Never feel that you are not deserving of help. We are all deserving of help and the angels love to help us.

There is nowhere, and no issue, that a teacher angel cannot help and no issue is too trivial for them to help with. A teacher angel can help you with whatever situation you are involved in. I know judges and surgeons who have called on a teacher angel to help them to do their job better. How wonderful to know that whatever situation we are in, we can always call on a teacher angel to come and teach us to cope better. We never need to feel hopeless. Teacher angels always bring hope.

I love gardening and have asked for a teacher angel to help when I'm doing the garden. I ask for teacher angels' help with everything in the garden, no matter how small the task. Sometimes it's so that I can tell the difference between plants and weeds; sometimes it's so that I can care for a particular plant in the best way possible, or to learn more about the creepy-crawlies that live on the ground and among the flowers and shrubs. Sometimes it's to help me learn how to do a particular task in a way that won't leave me with too many aches and pains afterwards.

My younger daughter Megan is fifteen. She was nervous recently before going to her first disco, so I suggested she asked for a teacher angel to help to teach her how to enjoy and have fun at her disco. She came home telling me that she had a brilliant time, and had lost all her anxieties. She was so looking forward to the next disco. Clearly her teacher angel had done a great job.

It's easy to ask for a teacher angel – just tell your guardian angel that you need help, and he will let a teacher angel in to help you. I keep saying I talk to angels the same way I talk to my friends – because they are my friends. You can do the same, talking to them silently or aloud. The important thing is to ask.

Once you have asked for a teacher angel to help you with learning a particular thing, then that teacher angel will come and go throughout your life when you need help with that subject.

You can also ask for a teacher angel to help someone else. Just ask your guardian angel for a teacher angel to help the person. Many parents have told me that they have asked for a teacher angel to help their children with their studying – this is so much better than fretting and worrying.

If you have already asked for a teacher angel, then do your best to listen and respond to the signs your teacher angel gives you. If you get an urge to turn the page of your book or to look up another book, do so. Or if a thought comes to your mind, write it down. Remember, you have nothing to lose, only to gain. Help your teacher angel to help you.

Your teacher angel isn't there to do all the work for you, though. You must play your part. If you have asked a teacher angel to help you with your exams you must play your part by doing the study. Your teacher angel will not do it for you. The teacher angel can help to give you confidence in your abilities, it can keep you focused so that you avoid distractions, and it can prompt you about what to study.

I remember walking past a group of students standing and chatting in the town. My attention was drawn to a young female student whom I had noticed a few days earlier studying, with a teacher angel beside her. Now, there were no teacher angels present; in general there are no teacher angels there when people are relaxing and having fun. Suddenly I saw her teacher angel appear and whisper in her ear. I overheard her saying she really needed to get back and do some study and as I walked slowly by I could hear her friends encouraging her to stay. As I continued walking I said a little prayer that she would listen to the teacher angel. When I reached the corner I glanced back and saw the young girl heading off without her friends in the direction of her college. She had listened and responded to her teacher angel.

I recently watched a little boy of about six playing football with friends on a green space. He had a teacher angel with him, who, I could tell from the ball he was holding, was obviously there to help him to learn football. The little boy had fallen and his friends were so engrossed in the game that they hadn't noticed and kept on playing. The little boy was rubbing his leg and the teacher angel was touching his leg at the same time as whispering in the little boy's ear that he would be OK and should get up and try again. The teacher angel bounced the ball gently beside the little boy, coaxing him up, and eventually the little boy struggled to his feet with his teacher angel beside him whispering encouragement all the time. I smiled because it was lovely to see the look of determination on this little boy's face as he responded to the angel's encouragement.

Then other little boys called out, asking whether he was OK, and kicked the football in his direction again. Even though I could see his leg was still hurting him, the young boy ran determinedly towards the football and gave it a really hard kick. The teacher angel kicked the football at the same time.

I asked the teacher angel, without words, whether this wasn't cheating. It smiled at me and replied that it was giving the little boy confidence in his own abilities, and that his next kick would be on his own. The little boy ran after the football, delighted with his kick. He had shown his friends he was as good a footballer as them.

Angels can teach us to do anything and – surprising as it may seem – they can also help us physically. When I go gardening, for example, I don't only have teacher angels; I also ask my guardian angel for angels to help me physically with the things that are physically challenging for me.

I see angels helping people physically all the time. Recently, I was walking down a street by a canal in Amsterdam after doing a speaking event and I saw two beautiful angels helping a man and woman who were coming out of a house with their arms full of cuttings from trees and shrubs. The man was dressed in worn working clothes – a jumper with a hole in it and tattered work trousers with frayed ends. He had an angel helping him. As the man wiped his brow, the angel that was with him did the same. This angel gave a male appearance, and I had to smile as he too looked as if he were in working clothes that were a bit torn and tattered. As the woman lifted and pushed the shrubs into the van, the angel with her was reflecting her movements. This woman clearly had asked for an angel to help her physically with her work.

In general, it is what I call unemployed angels who step in and help us physically when asked. I see so many unemployed angels around us. These are different to guardian angels or teacher angels but are angels who are available to help us any time we ask. I see so many of them that I always say there are millions of unemployed angels. These angels are white, and all look quite similar, although if I look closely I can see differences from one to another. Unemployed angels are very gentle and loving, so never be afraid to ask for their help physically – or to ask them to help someone you love. Again, all you have to do is ask your guardian angel to let some of the unemployed angels help you and it will.

I saw a lovely example of this from a taxi. My taxi had stopped near a junction and looking out the window I saw an elderly lady walking past, supported by a young man. Standing, bent over behind the elderly lady, was a large white angel helping her keep her balance. The elderly lady was very thin and stooped over with a curved back; she walked in a funny manner on legs as thin as matchsticks. But she was beautiful.

She walked with great determination, her body constantly shaking with the effort, lifting her legs like a solider marching. I could see she was a woman who lived life to the full and despite her physical difficulties she was enjoying her walk, no matter how hard it was.

There was another angel with them. This angel was constantly in front of her, waiting to catch her foot and guide it to the ground as she walked her funny walk. She must have asked her guardian angel for help, as unemployed angels cannot help us on their own – it's only when we ask that they can come and help us.

What made me smile even more was seeing the love and care the angels had for this elderly lady and her companion. I find it hard to understand sometimes why people are not more aware of the angels around them – the young man was completely unaware of the angels helping him and the elderly lady. I know we think we do everything on our own, but we don't. The angels constantly prove this to me. If the angels had not been there to help I doubt if the young man would have been able to support the elderly lady fully and she would have fallen.

Earlier today, as I was walking down to the town, I saw an elderly lady on the far side of the road. She had an angel walking along beside her, helping her to carry her shopping bag. This beautiful angel, dressed in a cream colour with a little gold, spoke to me, telling me that this lady asked God to send her an angel to help her physically every day. As the angel said these words, he reached out his other hand – the one not occupied in carrying shopping – and put it on the elderly lady's shoulder, massaging it to ease the strain. 'The bag is really very light for her, Lorna,' he told me. 'I am taking almost all of the weight.' The angel told me to look at her face. I was on the opposite side of the road but I could clearly see her smile. 'She knows you are helping her, doesn't she?' I asked the angel. He smiled and nodded.

There is an angel who sometimes helps the unemployed angels when we need help physically – the Angel of Strength.

I was on a bus one day and I watched a young man on crutches pull himself up onto the bus. On each side of him, helping to support him physically, were two unemployed angels. I could see their wings faintly and they were helping him with enormous gentleness and care. As the young man paid the driver, balancing one crutch under his arm and another against a seat, I asked God to send a special angel to help him. As I asked, a massive angel with a powerful masculine appearance of enormous strength appeared. This was the Angel of Strength. He always looks the same. He is enormous, and clear in colour, like clear water, although sometimes you might catch a glimpse of a golden streak within, like a golden thread running through him.

The Angel of Strength helps in a completely different way to any other angels. It is as if this amazing angel steps partially into a human body, as if in some ways the two bodies become one, but not quite. I watched as the Angel of Strength held on to the young man's body, as he stood there paying. It was as if the two bodies were merging, as if the Angel of Strength was pushing a mass of forceful strength into the young man's body.

As the boy hobbled on crutches down the aisle of the bus in the direction of my seat the massive angel was behind him, partially merged with him, and the two other angels were on either side still supporting him. Then, as the young man sat down a few seats ahead of me, aided by the two angels, it was as if he was sitting on the Angel of Strength and the angel had his arms wrapped tightly around him.

The Angel of Strength turned and looked back at me, saying, 'The young man is actually stronger than you think, Lorna. I will give him the courage and strength to fight to get completely well. I will help him until his full strength comes back into his legs and he is off crutches.' I was so pleased. I smiled at the Angel of Strength and thanked him. When the bus got to the terminus everyone got up to get off, except the young man. The Angel of Strength was whispering in his ear to wait and I could see that the young man was listening to this beautiful angel.

Another time, I saw the Angel of Strength helping a man at work in a garden. He was trying to pull a young tree out of the ground and to do it without damaging the roots so that he could replant the tree. He had already loosened a lot of the soil around the roots and I watched as he bent down to hold on to the base of the trunk to pull it out of the ground. The tree may have been young but it was still big and getting it out involved lots of hard physical work. The Angel of Strength was there helping him. The angel was directly behind him and moved as one with the man's body, pulling him backwards with a forceful strength. There were two other angels there giving the man encouragement, too – telling him to pull and that he could do it. He did – with the angels' help! All of a sudden the young tree broke through the soil and was free. The man laid it down on the ground and stood there wiping his brow and rubbing his hands. The Angel of Strength was still holding on to him tightly and, again, it was as if they were almost one body – but not quite. A beautiful sight to see. The man stood there looking very proud of himself, as if he had done it all on his own, and he called a woman – I presume his wife – who came out of the house to look at his handiwork.

Sometimes the Angel of Strength is called in when someone is worn out and exhausted and needs the strength and courage to go on. A few years ago, I was lent a house in Spain by a friend of mine and I and my two daughters, Ruth and Megan, went for a week's holiday. On a hot sunny day we were sitting at a table outside a café by the sea, enjoying the shade and watching the world go by. We were there about thirty minutes, sipping cool drinks, when the angels brought my attention to a man in working clothes, who was walking towards the café. He sat down at a table and ordered.

Megan and Ruth suggested a walk but the angels whispered to me that I should stay, so I did and the girls went off, leaving me on my own. The angels indicated that I should move my seat at the table so that I had a clear view of the man I had watched arrive a few minutes earlier.

I did so and I could see the man had his two hands together and bowed his head. I could see the Angels of Prayer were around him and I was allowed to hear his prayer. 'My God, please send me the strength to carry on with my work. I am so tired. I feel I can't go on.'

The waiter interrupted his prayer, putting a coffee down in front of him. At the same moment the Angel of Strength appeared directly behind the man. I was so happy to see God answering the man's prayer so quickly. And I prayed for him, too, and asked that the man would feel and see the difference.

The Angel of Strength was directly behind the man. Massive as always, he was about ten times bigger than the man. The man's and the angel's bodies were partially merged and it was as if the Angel of Strength was pouring strength and vitality into the man's body. He did it with such power – but such love and gentleness. It was beautiful to see the gentleness of this angel.

He talked to me without words. 'This man is exhausted. He is struggling so hard to farm the land on his own and he can't afford anyone to help. He is very worried about supporting his wife and young daughter. By the time he's finished his drink, he'll feel much stronger and more alive. He will have the physical and mental strength to go on. God has answered both his and your prayer.'

I was still there, waiting for the girls to come back, when the man got up and left. I could see the change in him by the way he walked and I said a prayer of thanks.

When you are exhausted or feeling physically challenged by a task, you can call on the Angel of Strength and ask for his help. He is one angel but he seems to be able to help many people at the one time. He won't stay with you, but will come and help you for that particular task where strength is needed. I have been asked how the Angel of Strength can be in different places at once – I don't know the answer. In this, the Angel of Strength is like the Angel of Hope or archangels – there is only one of them, but they can be in many different places at the same time.

You can, of course, also ask the Angel of Strength to help someone else.

I love walking and every chance I get I take some time and go for a walk. One day, a few years ago, I was out walking and passed a small Protestant church on the far side of the road. There were a few people coming out of the main door and some more walking slowly across the yard towards the gates of the church, chatting to each other. There were angels with them and, as always, I saw the light of their guardian angels right behind them. I wasn't really taking much notice but suddenly an angel called my name. It was Angel Hosus, one of the angels who has been a part of my life since childhood. He was beside me and he said, 'Stop and look over at the church again.'

As I stopped and looked I saw an angel walking out of the church. This angel was very tall and gave a female appearance. She was slender, radiant and translucent. This angel was much bigger than the arch and door of the church, and it was as if the arch and doorway weren't there for the angel. Instead, I saw something like a replica church in golden light that was much bigger than the physical church. The angel walked through the doorway of this bigger church. It may sound odd, but I could see this golden church at the same time as seeing the bricks and mortar of the physical church, but the golden church was more in proportion to the angel.

The angel stood in one spot in the yard in front of the church. Her clothing was made of what looked like lots of little mirrors of different sizes. The width of each panel of mirror varied but I could see such depth within each mirror. Her clothing was moving ever so gently as if there was a slight breeze around her. I could see the reverse side of some of the panels of mirror. It was like looking into another mirror full of life and depth. Taken all together the colour of the entire angel's clothing was like a white mirror reflecting little sparks of silver light. It was so beautiful to see.

Her eyes were like stars, shining with a glorious light but no colour. As she turned around on the same spot, to look around, it was as if I could see every part of the angel glimmering with light. Her hair was silver and short in length. It looked very untidy, sticking out from her head. In some places it looked as if her hair was standing on end.

For me the most incredible thing about this angel was her wings. Her wings were long, slender and enormous and they constantly moved as if they were breathing the air around them. At first I thought they were made of feathers, in the sense that we know feathers, but then the angel looked in my direction and stretched her wings out a little so that I could see them better. Her wings resembled feathers but they were made of delicate strands of mirror. The central stem of each 'feather' was turning constantly, reflecting a mirror of light. The 'feathers' were all different sizes. Some were long and narrow, and others started long and narrow and then halfway up became wider and more rounded. As the angel moved her wings they were giving flashes of brilliant light, which were dazzling.

Then a beam of light seemed to come from above the trees that surrounded the little green to the left of the church. The beam of light hit the angel as she started to move upwards into the sky. When the angel and the beam of light were above the church they disappeared.

I stood there, across from the church, looking, and then turned to Hosus, who had been beside me all the time. 'Hosus, who is that angel?' I asked. Hosus smiled at me, but gave me no answer. He told me to enjoy my walk as he disappeared, touching my cheek and telling me to smile. I looked back at the little church and realised that all the people were gone. I walked away asking God who the angel was, but He gave me no answer either.

I believe, though, that this is an angel that I will meet again, that this is an angel who has come to help me with some aspect of my life in the future. I have often been introduced to angels in this way, and not been told how they would help me, and then years later I have discovered the part they will play.

You may not see angels but I know God sends special angels into certain people's lives at certain times to help with extraordinary circumstances.

Angels are such a sign of hope. There is always an angel that can help us, regardless of what is going on in our lives. All we have to do is ask. You don't need to know what angel to ask for; just ask and your guardian angel will call in the help you need. Isn't it wonderful to know that there is such an abundance of help there? To me it seems so strange, and sad, that so many people don't make use of this gift.

CHAPTER FOUR

Parenting is the most important job in the world

I AM A SINGLE PARENT. MY HUSBAND JOE DIED after a long illness, leaving me with four children, the youngest of whom was only four, and I know how hard it is to be a single parent. I pray to God often to help me to be the best parent possible to my children, especially my youngest who is now only fifteen and doing state exams for the first time. My son Owen and my daughter Ruth are now parents themselves and are already finding it challenging, even though they of course love being parents. A parent's job is never-ending, regardless of your children's age.

Parenting is the most important job in the world. Being a parent is to me more important than any other role in my life. God and the angels have given me the task of spreading the message that everyone has a guardian angel, and that everyone has a soul, and to help me in this task God has allowed me to see angels physically. But still, for me, the most important role or destiny in my life is to be a mother, the parent to my four children. I know many people will be shocked to hear me say this but God has entrusted me with four children and I have to rear them, protect them, support them and they will always come first. Let me say it again. Parenting is the most important job in the world.

Being a parent is not easy. It's one of the hardest and most challenging tasks of all and it is for ever. Your children may grow up, and become parents themselves, but you continue to be their mother or father.

When I talk of the importance of parents I don't just mean biological parents. I include adopted parents, long-term foster parents or anyone who has been asked to be the primary carer of a child. Lots of other people help in the parenting of a child: friends, aunts, uncles and grandparents are very important. But there is a real difference between people who help and support a child and the primary carer – the person or people who have no one to give the child back to if things get tough. When God gives you a child you must take responsibility for that child. God trusts you to be the best possible carer of that child.

On many occasions mothers have asked me questions like, 'What is my destiny?' or 'What is my life purpose?' Sometimes they will ask this with a child on their knee and their arms around it. My heart cries out when I am asked this and fills with compassion for the mother, and I pray in silence, 'God, does she not realise what she holds in her arms? Her child!'

My answer to any mother who would ask this question is this: 'Look at your beautiful children. Your first, most important and greatest destiny is to be a mother to your children. To turn your children into kind, loving, caring members of the community, who know right from wrong. You are moulding and shaping your children to be the future teachers, nurses, doctors and leaders. Whatever your child does – even the most basic job – if you have reared them well they will be capable of making an important contribution. You shape the future of the world, because you shape your children, who are a part of the future.'

I feel so sad when I discuss this with parents and they tell me something like, 'They are just my children. They are not part of my destiny. There has got to be a greater purpose to my life.'

Many parents think that their children are stopping them from living a more fulfilled life. But your children bring you out into the world, they make you more aware of the world around you and it is through being a parent that many people get more involved in the world around them and learn much more about themselves. Sometimes people talk as if an individual has only one destiny or purpose in life, but in fact we all have many purposes in our lives and being a parent is the most important one.

Alongside being a parent we all have other things we are called upon to do, like being a good neighbour or earning a living. I am called to write these books and pass on all the messages that God and the angels have given me. This is a demanding task and one it is important for me to fulfil. Parents can and do do other things to use their gifts in the world. It is important to use the gifts and talents that you are given, partly because in this way you give an example to your children of how to live their lives to the full.

I have been struggling a bit with writing this chapter and I have been asking Angel Michael for help. Angel Michael is one of the angels who has been a part of my life since childhood. The first time I saw him I was about five. He looked like other angels, but there was something different about him; he shone more strongly than the others and he had a commanding presence, a powerful force of male strength. From that first time I saw him I always felt he was ready to protect me, like a shield, and from then on he kept appearing and gradually we became friends. He told me his name was Michael. Many years later he told me that he was the Archangel Michael.

 Your child has chosen you as its mother or father.

I have been trying to find a way to explain just how important being a parent is. Angel Michael has told me to remind you that your child chose you as its parent, just as Jesus chose Holy Mary to be his mother and Joseph to be his father on this earth.

Your child has chosen you as its mother or father. Hard as you might find this to believe, your child – when it was still a soul in Heaven, before it was conceived – chose *you* to be its parent. It chose you, knowing everything about you, the good and the bad. Even knowing that you might not be the best father or mother, it chose you over all others. I can't explain why unborn souls choose a particular parent – why did my children choose me and Joe?

Babies also choose adoptive or long-term foster parents. Sometimes a soul will have chosen more than two parents, knowing that a parent might die or be unable to rear it.

At a book signing in Belfast, a young couple in their late twenties came up to me. There were loads of angels around them but the light of their guardian angels hadn't opened – yet. The husband, looking emotional, burst out, 'We are trying to adopt because we can't have children of our own.' As he said this, his wife started to cry. A beautiful angel to her right bent over her, hugging her as she wept. Her husband tried to console her. He asked me to pray that their adoption application would be approved. The young woman grabbed my hands and said, 'Lorna, please ask God to grant us a baby. We want a family. We'll be really good parents – the best.' Her husband nodded beside her.

'I will pray and ask,' I promised. 'Keep asking the guardian angels of all the people in the adoption process to help to send you a child.'

The man looked at me, saying, 'We don't care what age or nationality or whether it's boy or a girl – we want a child of our own – it will be ours.' I blessed and prayed over them.

I watched as they walked away from the table where

I was signing, arms around each other. The light of the guardian angel behind both of them opened up, shielding my view of them for a moment, and from the back I saw two beautiful guardian angels, significantly taller than the husband and wife, glowing like gold. Both guardian angels gave a male appearance. They seemed to be wearing long cloaks of gold, which had perfect pleats. They had wings that were closed and they didn't show me their wings fully. As the couple walked away, arm in arm and escorted by their angels, I was told that their baby had already chosen them and was waiting for them.

When I come across people with problems having a baby I always tell them not to give up. Infertility does not mean that a soul hasn't chosen you to be its mother or father. Listen to your guardian angel and see what promptings you are being given. I met a mother in Kilkenny recently and she told me that she and her husband had decided to adopt a baby from Romania. They went to Romania understanding they were getting a baby under six months old. In the orphanage, the woman in charge took them into a yard where there were three- to five-year-olds playing and tried to give them one of these children. The couple kept protesting that they were there for a baby, and she kept shrugging and saying, 'No babies, only these babies.' This went on for a while with the adoptive parents getting increasingly upset. A series of children were paraded in front of them.

Out of the corner of her eye the mother-to-be started to watch a ragged little girl who was standing on her own by a swing, wailing. She felt drawn to this child. The parents had never considered the idea of adopting a three-year-old, let alone a three-year-old who had suffered mental and emotional damage and who would never be completely able for this world. Yet, to their surprise, they chose this terrified three-year-old, who was afraid to even hug them and who screamed all the time.

This little soul had chosen them as her parents before she was born and they had listened to God and their guardian angels and recognised her. When the mother told me this, the child had been in Ireland a few years. She still had a lot of difficulties and she still had special needs but with her parents' love and patience she was now able to express affection.

The angels with me whispered in my ear to ask the mother whether she would make the same choice again. She looked at me, surprised, and considered carefully before answering, 'I can't imagine life without her. Life isn't easy now, and it never will be as she will always need our help. But we love her, she's our daughter and with our love hopefully she will grow into a loving gentle adult.'

Years ago, when Ruth was only a baby, Angel Michael told me that I would write a book about God and the angels. When I protested that I couldn't read or write properly he told me that help would be sent and, years later, after my husband died, that help materialised in my friend and agent, Jean. Some years later, down in Johnstown, Angel Michael told me that Jean wasn't just there to help me get the message of God and the angels out into the world, but that she was also there to play a special and important role for my daughter, Megan. Jean was there to help Megan to realise her talents and her potential in the world. It has been wonderful to see this unfolding in the nine years that Jean has been in Megan's life. Megan was six when they met for the first time. Her brothers and sister, of course, play an important part, but Jean's role is completely different. Jean – as someone well educated and well travelled – is able to open Megan's eyes to things in a way I couldn't (Megan calls Jean 'an encyclopedia!') and is an important influence on her as well as being a special friend to her.

Throughout my children's lives I can see the

influence and help that different adults have given. My eldest son, Christopher, for example, benefited enormously from the friendship and support of the father of one of his friends. This man took a particular interest in Christopher at a time when his own father, Joe, was sick. This man helped Christopher to recognise his talents and decide that he should study engineering. I will always be grateful to this man, and to other adults who have helped my children, for their help and support. As I often say, I can't do everything on my own and no parent can.

The angels put adults into children's lives. Sometimes this is just for a short period – a word of encouragement – and sometimes it's for longer. The angels tell me that every adult needs to play their part with the young people around them. Parents may have the most important role, but for our children to grow up as they should the angels tell me that they need the friendship, attention and support of adults other than their parents around them.

I was up at the stables where Megan does her horse riding the other day. One of the women there was pregnant. She was surrounded by angels – other than her guardian angel – and they were dancing around her full of joy, so excited about this little baby who was to be born in about a month. For a moment I could see the infant inside of her and I was shown the love that the baby had for its mother; its joy feeling the way its mother was protecting it and keeping it safe. Your child loves you long before it is born.

Sometimes when I am shown a baby in its mother's tummy the angels around the mother will tell me that this little baby is not going to stay. When an angel tells me this I understand there will be a miscarriage. Despite this, the angels show me all the love that this tiny baby is pouring out on the mother it has chosen. The soul chose this mother and father even knowing it will not be born. I have asked God and the angels why this happens, why a mother miscarries. They haven't answered me fully. They have told me it is primarily to do with the life path of that little soul, short as it is, rather than that of the parents. But the soul of this little baby loves its parents so deeply that it stays around them after death to help to comfort them and ease the pain of their loss. That little soul loves its parents so much that it's there for them when they need it. The baby has, of course, gone to Heaven and is happy but, hard as this might be to understand, it can be with the parents at the same time as being in Heaven.

The same is true for any baby that has been aborted. At a signing recently, a young woman told me of an abortion she had had some years before. As she sat in front of me in tears, I was shown the spirit of a baby boy on her lap. The expression of love on the face of the spirit baby boy was so moving. I could see its unconditional love for its mother. It had chosen her knowing that there would be an abortion.

I meet lots of parents and they frequently ask how they can be a better mother or father. Many men in particular tell me that they think they are no good at being fathers. A man in his thirties came up to me in a hotel in London once and asked for a few moments of my time. The angels whispered in my ear to give him a few minutes, so I looked around the hotel and suggested a quiet table by the window. He told me he believed he wasn't a good father, and this was really worrying him and causing him a lot of stress.

'I have a seven-year-old girl and a ten-year-old boy,' he told me. 'I treat my son as if he is stupid, even though I know he probably isn't. I run him down and do exactly what my father did to me: my father used to compare me with his friends' sons. I feel really bad about it, but I don't seem to be able to help it.'

He told me that when he came in from work he would go and talk to his son as he was doing his homework and would look through his exercise books, pointing out where he had a spelling wrong. Or would ask him to read aloud and then get impatient that he wasn't fast enough or was making mistakes with pronunciation. 'My dad did exactly that with me, finding faults all the time. He made me into a nervous wreck and now I'm doing the same thing with my own son.'

He had tears in his eyes, which he tried to hide with his hand up to his face, as he asked, 'How can I change this, Lorna?'

I looked at him and said, 'Remember, your father did his best. He wasn't perfect. No father is, and he could only do his best. But you recognise that his was not the best way, that he made mistakes and you want to do better and that makes you a good father already – even if you don't believe it. Ask your guardian angel to help you and your son to become friends. Your son loves you, and you love both him and your daughter.'

As I said these words the light of his guardian angel opened for a moment and embraced him. His guardian angel spoke to me without words, in such a compassionate and loving way, telling me to keep on encouraging him, that he already was a good father.

'Ask your guardian angel to help you to be patient with your son,' I continued. 'Remember, he is only a child and has an awful lot to learn. When you are looking at your son's homework find the things he has done well. Let your son know you are very proud of him. Most important of all, spend more time playing with your son and your daughter, and listen attentively to them when they are telling you something. That way, as they grow, they will share with you their worries and troubles and will never be afraid to come to you with their problems.'

The man sat there wiping his eyes. 'You will have a brilliant relationship with your children,' I continued, 'even when they are adults, and you are a grandfather.' The man smiled at me, saying, 'I am so sorry for being so emotional. I have never cried in public like this before.'

I smiled and told him not to worry, that it happened around me a lot. 'Just remember,' I said as I leaned over to bless him, 'ask your guardian angel to help you to become a brilliant father and ask your children's guardian angels to help, too.'

Many parents have become conscious that both they and their children have a guardian angel who never leaves them for one second and that they can ask their own guardian angel to ask their children's guardian angels to help their children. Lots of mothers tell me that they remind their children that they have a guardian angel as they go out the door to school in the morning. They tell me that they also ask the children's guardian angels to look after them at school and help them with their work and play.

Many mothers and fathers have told me that knowing that both they and their children have a guardian angel has made them better parents, that knowing that there are angels there to help has made life easier and has guided them to be better parents. They tell me that when they find themselves getting irritated or stressed they become conscious of the promptings of their guardian angel, telling them to be patient, and they feel themselves relaxing and becoming more loving and their homes more full of joy.

I know from my own personal experience that being a parent is not easy. In fact, at times it's extremely stressful, but remember, being a parent is the most important job in the world.

CHAPTER FIVE

Prayer can move mountains

PRAYER IS SUCH A POWERFUL FORCE. WE UNDER-
estimate it so much. Prayer can move mountains if
only we would let it. If only you would realise just
how powerful prayer can be, you will never feel
hopeless.

You may think you don't pray very much. You may
think you don't pray at all. But a prayer can be a quick
thought that crosses your mind, a word or a cry to
God for help. Even what we might think of as swearing
can sometimes in fact be a prayer – if it comes from
the soul.

I talk and ask the angels to help; I ask angels to

intercede but I don't pray to them. I pray only to God. Prayer is direct communication with God.

No one ever prays alone. When you pray to God there are a multitude of angels of prayer there, praying with you, regardless of your religious faith or how you are behaving. They are there enhancing your prayer, interceding on your behalf and imploring God to grant your prayer. Every time you pray, even if it is only one word, the angels of prayer are like a never-ending stream flowing at tremendous speed to Heaven with your prayers.

Angels of prayer are very hard to describe, particularly as when I see them it is generally as a flow of hundreds of thousands of them in a stream of light. It's a constantly moving light a bit like a waterfall falling from a height, except it's flowing upwards. I rarely see angels of prayer standing still but let me describe one from a time when I did. Angels of prayer are extremely tall, much taller than any person, with long and slender wings which seem to be in constant motion. They don't give an appearance of being male or female but are surrounded by a shimmering light, which glimmers like sunshine. They wear flowing white robes that are loose. Sometimes when they are moving I will see a glimpse of another colour but it's always very subtle. Angels of prayer are extremely beautiful.

I know it's hard to believe that I see hundreds of thousands of angels of prayer flowing like a river towards Heaven, bringing a person's prayers and presenting them at the throne of God. But that is what I am shown; it's as if angels of prayer bring every bit of the prayer – every syllable that is prayed for – up to Heaven. When the person stops praying, the flow stops, but as soon as the person starts to pray again, the stream of angels of prayer resumes.

People sometimes ask me how to pray. Let me start by telling you how I learnt to pray as a young child. I was taught to pray by a special angel when I was about four years old. This was the Angel Amen – although I only knew her as 'the special angel of prayer' until years later.

The Angel Amen used to come and sit on my bed with me and teach me how to pray. She used to sit on my bed like a teenager, with crossed legs covered by a full skirt. Angel Amen gave me the appearance of a beautiful young woman with long, honey-blonde hair with curls. My curls had been cut off shortly before I met Angel Amen for the first time, so I was particularly impressed by her hair. Her clothes were made of an embroidered cream fabric, like a fine silk. There were patterns embroidered on the silk but I have no idea, even now, what they symbolised. Her dress was very shapely to her waist, but the skirt that fell to her ankles was very full. The sleeves were long and wide.

Angel Amen never came when there was anyone else in the bedroom I shared with my sister Emer, who was two years older than me. Mostly she came when I was in bed ready for sleep but sometimes she appeared during the day when I was playing in the room on my own.

She would take my hand and guide it to make the sign of the cross. She was showing me a Christian symbol as I was born a Catholic. If I was born into another religious tradition I know she would have taught me what was important to that tradition.

She taught me to pray to God using my normal everyday words and she also taught me how to say some of the formal prayers of the Catholic Church, like the Hail Mary and the Our Father. I would, of course, later learn these in school.

Sometimes she would tell me to close my eyes and other times she would tell me to look at her. She taught me some special prayers that she told me I was never to share with anyone. It's very strange but I seem to have forgotten them as I grew older – I know that Angel Amen has hidden them from me.

Angel Amen taught me a particular form of meditative prayer, where I pray with every particle of my body and my soul. This is very intensive and deep prayer and since I was a child I have prayed like this for some time every day. Sometimes it's just for a few minutes – sometimes it's longer – but when I pray like this it's as if time has no meaning and I feel tremendous joy.

Angel Amen also taught me how to have my soul in constant prayer – even when I am doing something else. Even now, as I am writing this, I am praying for things I have been asked to pray for. It's a bit hard to explain how I can be doing both at the same time – but I am.

Angel Amen did most of her teaching with me when I was between four and six years old. Then she came to me regularly. Now she comes to me about once a month. I love it when Angel Amen comes to pray with me. When she takes my hand she fills me with so much peace and each word as we pray is so slow and so long. I don't know exactly why she comes but I believe it's because her presence enhances my prayers. When she comes to pray with me, I seem to remember those special prayers she taught me again. The following morning, though, I will have no memory of the words of them.

Angel Amen has a very important part to play in helping the world to pray – regardless of religion or beliefs. The word 'Amen' is like the beginning and end of any prayer. It's a very important word. Try to use the word 'Amen' at the end of your prayer. It enhances your prayer. That's why God put it there in the first place. But don't worry if you forget to say 'Amen'. The angels of prayer will say it for you.

I know everyone can learn how to pray and if you ask the Angel Amen, she will help you. You might just say, 'Angel Amen, please teach me how to pray.'

Try and get into the habit of saying even a little prayer. It might be while you are standing at your kitchen sink looking out the window, or walking along a road. Perhaps say a little prayer for something that you are worried about, something you saw or heard on the news or something you are grateful for – nothing is too big or too small to pray about. Start to take a moment every day to pray, knowing that the angels of prayer will be right there with you.

It can be as simple and short a prayer as, 'God, help me. Amen.'

You will be amazed at the difference even saying a small prayer can make. Over time, praying – even for a very short moment each day – will give you such a feeling of peace. As you pray, try and become aware that you have a soul, that there is more to you than just your flesh and blood. Ask God to make you more connected to your soul, so that your body and soul become one in prayer. As you pray more, you will become more spiritual and you will feel yourself lifted spiritually. I know that if even for one second you felt the connection between your soul and yourself it would give you a feeling of such joy.

Some people like to pray using formal prayers, like the Our Father, but you can also pray just by talking to God as you would a friend, asking for help. Sometimes we feel we can't find the right words to pray, or that our words aren't good enough. Whatever words you use – they are good enough and the angels of prayer enhance them. There is nothing too small to pray for.

Sometimes, the angels allow me to hear someone at prayer: a mother saying a quick prayer in a church, while her children are running around, that the children would sleep tonight. A young man at the bus stop, praying for the bus to hurry up. People pray about the ordinary concerns of everyday life and it's great to see.

Angel Michael has always told me that while there are different religions, there is only one God and that in the future all religions should become unified under one umbrella. He has also told me that the prayers of people of all religions are equally powerful.

Nothing is too big to pray for either. Sometimes, we get overwhelmed by a situation such as a war or a famine and feel we can do nothing to help. We can. We can pray. We shouldn't ever doubt the power of prayer. When we are moved by something we see on the TV news or read about in a newspaper we should say a prayer. Any feeling of sadness or compassion inside of us is in fact a type of prayer. But it becomes much bigger if we do acknowledge it in the form of prayer.

When you hear an ambulance or walk past a hospital, say a quick prayer for whoever is sick and for those who are caring for them. When you see someone in difficulties on the street, say a prayer for them. We all need to expand our circle of prayers out from ourselves, our family and friends. You are being called upon to pray for other people – including people in the world whom you have never met.

We need to pray for our communities and our leaders – politicians, business leaders, church leaders, community leaders. We all need to pray that they will listen to God and his angels and make the right decisions, as their decisions affect all of us.

> **I believe that each and every one of you has been demonstrated the power of prayer in your own life.**

Too often, we forget to say thank you, to say a prayer of gratitude. When we do, it helps us to appreciate more the blessings we have received and deepens and strengthens our faith and our relationship with God. Saying prayers of gratitude helps us to realise how much we actually have and gives us hope and confidence for the future.

I wanted to include some special prayers in this book and asked Angel Amen to come to help me. I was working at the computer and she appeared beside me, squatted down and said some words of prayer, which seemed to me to take only a few moments – but I know it must have been longer. Then she disappeared. I was very anxious that I would forget the prayer but Angel Hosus came and helped me to remember the words that Angel Amen had given me to share with you. It's a prayer of thanks to God.

A Prayer of Thanks

*Thank you for all the blessings you have
    bestowed upon me, my God.*
*The blessing of having a soul, that speck of
    your light;*
*The blessing of the gift of my guardian
    angel for eternity, who never leaves me
    even for one second;*
*The blessing of the peace and love that
    dwell in me;*
The blessing of the family you have given me;
*The blessing of those you send into my life
    for companionship;*
*The blessing of living in harmony with
    those around me;*
The blessing of my labour, my work;
*The blessings of all the material things I
    have in my life, big and small;*
*The blessings of this wonderful world and
    the nature around me.*
*Thank you, my God, for all the things I
    forget to thank you for.*
*And most of all, thank you, my God, for
    continuing to bless my life.*
Amen.

Praying with others is very powerful, particularly when a community is praying together for the same cause. When I am at Mass, which is the form of group prayer I am most familiar with, most of the time I am shown that people are praying for their own needs and those of their family and friends. But when there is a request to pray for a particular group or need, and most people turn their prayer to that intention, I see an intensification of the prayer – I see more and more angels of prayer flowing to Heaven.

The Angel Amen has told me that when people of different religions pray together it is particularly powerful.

Every time I go into a church, mosque, synagogue or temple – or any holy place – I see hundreds of angels praying, quite aside and separate from any angel of prayer. It doesn't matter what religion the place belongs to – if any. Whether it's a building or a space outside, even if the place is no longer being used for prayer, it is still a holy place, and there will be angels there, praying to God.

Any spot where someone prays can become a holy place – a particular room, a chair in your house or a corner in the park. It's as if, when you pray there regularly, the angels of prayer leave something behind there and that particular spot becomes more peaceful or calmer. This is one of the reasons that many people find it easier to pray in the same place whenever possible.

Many of us use material things to help us to pray. Some of us use beads, prayer books or incense or we light candles. These things are symbols and are treated as holy by different religious traditions. They help us to connect to God, but we should remember it is we who need them, not God. Candles are, of course, a symbol of hope, a symbol of the light of God. People light candles for so many different reasons. One of my favourites is when people light a candle at home to make their home a holy place, a place of peace and love.

I love to pray with others, of any religion. I get great joy out of it; I get such power and energy out of it – it's as if it lifts my soul and my soul dances.

I long for the day when people of all religions will pray together more. Recently, when in the United States, I had the honour of being invited to speak at a big Catholic conference in San Francisco, to pray in a mosque in New York and also to pray with a Hindu community. The three-day conference in San Francisco was a great treat: there was so much praying over three days – and not just during Mass or when formal prayers were being said. While I was being interviewed in front of the audience I would suddenly see a flash of angels of prayer rising from someone and I would know they had just said a prayer.

I'm going to tell you about what I saw at a Mass at this conference, but, of course, I see similar things at Mass in my own local church or in any other part of the world when I have attended Mass.

As Mass began in the big conference room the light of the guardian angels behind everyone became bright. There were also many angels on the makeshift altar. It was a big stage but it seemed enormous given the number of angels on it. There were two huge angels on either side of the priest. As the priest lifted the Host an enormous angel seemed to come through his body and lift the Host with the priest and then took it to Heaven in a flash. It was absolutely beautiful to watch. At the same moment as the angel carried the Host up to Heaven, the light of the Holy Spirit came down and into the Host, infusing it with God's grace. As people went up for Communion there were two angels on either side of the priest enhancing the Host as the people were receiving Communion.

Recently, as I said, I was invited to pray in a mosque in New York. Although the mosque was quite full with people – perhaps 500 men and 50 women – the place was packed with thousands and thousands of angels. It was as if they filled every available space and it was beautiful to see how, as the men and women knelt in prostration, the angels bowed down in the same way. The community was so engrossed in their prayer, so concentrated on it, that the glow of the angels of prayer constantly flowing to Heaven gave a glow to the room. As the imam spoke, encouraging and giving hope to the congregation, he was surrounded by very tall angels. They all gave a male appearance and seemed to be dressed in robes that I could imagine priests wearing centuries ago. One beautiful angel was very prominent. It wasn't the imam's guardian angel. This angel was very tall and blocky, and his robes were heavy, and I saw gold in them. I could see no wings. His head looked big and masculine and on it was some sort of unusual hat. It wasn't quite round and was flat at the front. He had his hand gently on each of the imam's shoulders – as if steadying him with gentleness and care. He seemed to be speaking to him all the time.

I hope very much that in the future I will be invited to pray with more congregations of different faiths and pray that in the future we will all pray together more. Prayer is a powerful force for good in this world.

We could do so much if we acknowledged this and prayed together. Imagine if everyone in the world, regardless of religion, agreed to stop what they were doing and pray for a few minutes every day at a certain time. The impact of humanity acting as one in prayer would be enormous for our world.

I see the power of prayer every day in the world; I see miracles happening because of it, but I can't explain it or prove it. Prayer works in mysterious ways and we are not conscious of much of the things that happen as the result of prayer.

I believe miracles happen every day but we don't see them most of the time. A lot of these are small miracles but they can make a major change within an individual's or a family's life.

I believe that each and every one of you has been demonstrated the power of prayer in your own life. I believe that every one of you has been prayed for on occasions by others – even people who are completely unknown to you – and that you have benefited from it. Our prayers are always answered but not always answered in the way we think they should be. God and the angels assure me that no prayer goes unheard or unheeded. It's very hard for us to understand how we can pray for someone to get well, and then they die. Why weren't our prayers answered? Why are our prayers for people who are starving on the other side of the world not answered?

I understand people asking these questions.

In thinking, talking and praying about these questions as I write this chapter, I have realised that there are four main reasons why people feel that their prayers are not answered.

Sometimes we pray for something that is not part of God's plan, so perhaps a loved one doesn't get well because it's time for them to go home to God.

Sometimes we pray for things we want and believe we should get and are disappointed when we don't get them. We are often blinded by our desire for whatever it is we think we need but often we don't recognise fully what will be best for us. Often, with hindsight, we say we are glad that we didn't get something that we had previously prayed for.

Sometimes our prayers are not answered because we or other people let the other side in – we let evil in. This is how war can start and continue despite our prayers.

The fourth reason I think of is that people have not listened and taken action. This may be through fear – fear of being ridiculed, fear of poverty, fear of failure – or complacency. God and the angels need us to achieve things in the world. Yes we need to pray, but we need action as well. Each and every one of us has a part to play.

We need to have faith and keep praying, even if our faith in the power of prayer is challenged at times. In fact, it will always be challenged because we will never have a full understanding of God's vision for our world.

We may not always see the results of our prayers but whether we see it or not we have to have faith that they are making a difference to our lives and to the world as a whole. Prayer gives hope – sometimes all we have is this hope.

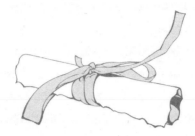

CHAPTER SIX

We all have the grace of healing within us

I WAS WALKING DOWN THE CORRIDOR OF A hospice in Dublin, having visited a friend. Two women were sitting on the wide window sill and a man was standing with them. I could see the light of their guardian angels behind them but no other angels. The door to the room opposite them was closed, as this was a room for people who were near death. I knew they were a grieving family and friends. I could see a special energy coming from each of them and going to the others. I was being shown the grace of healing. I saw a wave of energy that came from every part of their bodies. It came with a force, but also gentleness.

The grace of healing is different to any other energy I see, and as I walked past I could feel the tremendous stillness and calmness that I always feel from it. The energy wasn't going in the direction of the room where their loved one was dying. Instead, it was being shared among the three people there, helping to ease their pain and grief.

Each and every one of us has the grace of healing within us – and it is a wonderful gift God has given us. I see it at work every day. It's beautiful when I see a mother or father holding a child in their arms and comforting them. The child might have a physical hurt, like a scratched knee, or an emotional hurt like sadness, but the parent, usually unbeknown to him or herself, is pouring out the grace of healing. It is wonderful to see the grace of healing flow from the parent to the child and to see the child stop crying and go back to playing happily.

Children use the grace of healing among themselves. One child will get hurt when a group is playing, and the other children will come and fuss over him, showing their concern and love. Then the hurt child forgets his pain and goes back to playing. We see the grace of healing at work all the time, but most of us don't recognise it.

This is not just about parents and children. Every one of us has the grace of healing within us. Whenever you feel moved to help someone who is hurting – someone you love or someone you have never even met – you are using the grace of healing. Love and compassion release the healing power that is within you. Ever since I was a child, Angel Michael has told me that love is the force behind the grace of healing.

I haven't talked much about this healing grace before. I use healing grace constantly, with people I meet going down the street or shopping in the super-market. To me it's so natural that I am a bit surprised when people ask me about it.

As I have been working on this chapter it has been pointed out to me that the way I talk about the grace of healing sounds a lot like what I have said about the power of both prayer and love. I can understand this, because prayer and love have healing aspects to them as well. But I see the grace of healing that is within each and every one of us as different to prayer or love, although they are all linked. The only way I can explain the grace of healing is that it is a power that comes from your soul into your body to help you to heal yourself and others.

We all have the grace of healing within us; it is completely natural and we do it instinctively – we just don't automatically recognise it within ourselves. I see people using the grace of healing all the time but 99 per cent of the time I know that the person is not aware that they are sending healing. When the person is conscious of using the grace of healing it appears to me to be intensified.

Through becoming aware that you have the grace of healing within you, and having the intention to use it, you will learn how to release it. As you become more conscious of it you will be surprised at the difference it can make. This is not about people becoming healers. It's about people in their everyday lives becoming conscious of this grace and using it to send healing in ordinary situations – to the woman down the road who had a hip replacement, to your sister with a headache, to a colleague who is stressed out. Some people like to do this by visualising healing grace flowing towards the person but I personally don't use visualisations.

Surprising as it may seem, we can use the grace of healing with our pets as well. When a much-loved animal becomes sick you can allow the grace of healing to help your pet get well. I love animals and over the years have had a lot of pets. I have simply done it by holding them and stroking them and talking softly to them.

God has given us the gift of the grace of healing to use for ourselves. So why wouldn't we use it? When I see someone using healing grace for themselves it looks like a wave coming from the whole of the body – from the toes to the top of the head, it flows out to about one foot away from the body and then like a wave breaking turns back and fills the whole body it has come from. When it re-enters the body I see it flowing like a river, like a line of gold towards the part of the body that needs help.

Become conscious of the healing grace coming from you and instead of directing it to others, turn it back on yourself and let it fill you like a wave of peace. It sounds complicated, but in fact it's quite simple and many people do it instinctively. Try and become more conscious of using healing grace for yourself and get into the habit of using it no matter how trivial the hurt, emotional or physical, may seem. Remember, there is an abundance of healing grace; using it for yourself does not mean there is less for someone else.

Too often we lack compassion for ourselves and are very judgmental. I meet many people who hate themselves physically; they won't allow themselves to see the beauty of their bodies. Whether we believe it or not we are all perfect. What you perceive as faults are not faults. They are a part of the unique being that is you.

When a person becomes conscious of this healing grace within themselves they start to see themselves differently. Get into the habit every day of taking ten seconds to acknowledge the healing grace within yourself and feel its power at work within you. Your guardian angel will help, too. Ask to become more conscious of the power of the grace of healing within you so that you will allow it to flow through you for the healing you need.

> **God has given us the gift of the grace of healing to use for ourselves. So why wouldn't we use it?**

At a book signing a woman came up to me. She took a deep breath and said, 'I need to ask you about my daughter.' As she said this she looked over at a little girl of about four who was playing with her younger brother over by the children's books. There were about five healing angels circling the little girl. Healing angels always seem to work in small groups and encircle the person they are healing. Healing angels look similar to each other, but when you look closely you realise that they are all different in subtle ways. They are slender and very tall, generally three of four feet taller than the person they are surrounding. The give no appearance of being either male or female. As with all angels, they are extremely beautiful. Their clothing, which covers them from head to toe, radiates a crystal-clear light of a perfect white-silver colour. Their wings are faint and move gently all the time, as if moving in a gentle breeze.

Generally, healing angels are only there for a fleeting moment. They never seem to stay any length of time with a sick person. They seem to come and go as the healing is needed. On this day they stayed there for an unusually long time.

Healing angels use the same grace of healing that each and every one of us has, but it's more powerful as their healing grace comes directly from God. God pours a beam of healing light down onto the healing angels and through touch the healing angels pass God's healing on to us. Healing angels are unusual in this because most angels don't touch us.

God allows healing angels to intervene when asked and when there is serious illness involved. I have never seen healing angels where an injury has been minor. Seeing the healing angels with the little girl there I knew the mother's worries were justified. I moved closer to the mother and took her hand saying, 'Tell me what's worrying you.'

One of the healing angels from around the little girl came over and stood beside the mother. This was unusual. I have rarely seen a healing angel leave the group. The mother continued, 'Sometimes I get a feeling that my little girl is not well, that something is wrong with her.'

As the mother said this, the healing angel standing beside her touched the mother's shoulder and spoke to me without words. 'Lorna, tell her to take the child to the doctor.'

Again, without words, I asked the angel, 'Is it life threatening?'

'No, Lorna,' the angel replied, 'it's serious but she will get well.'

I asked the mother, 'Have you been praying for your daughter?'

The mother looked at me and said, 'How did you know that?'

I smiled at her. 'That is why your daughter is surrounded by healing angels. You asked God for help and God sent healing angels to be with your daughter. The healing angels are the ones who keep prompting you with the feeling that your child is unwell.'

The mother told me that she had taken her daughter

to the doctor but he had said there was nothing wrong. She felt there was, though.

'The angels are telling me that you must take your little girl back to the doctor and get him to do some blood tests. There is something wrong that needs to be attended to, but don't worry, I know your little girl will be OK. Trust the feelings you get inside of you and listen. It's the healing angels who have been prompting you. I know you listen because you came here to talk to me today. Remember, you can help to heal your daughter; you need to go to the doctor, but you also have the grace of healing within you. Cuddle her and be conscious of allowing the grace of healing within you to pour out on to her. This will help her to get well faster.'

As I said goodbye to her, her children came over, I blessed them and their mother and asked the healing angels to help the little girl get well as quickly as possible. I watched them walk away and I could see the light of their guardian angels behind each of them. The healing angels had already disappeared.

Often, when I talk about healing angels and using the healing grace that is inside all of us, people ask why it is that some people get better and others don't. My husband Joe suffered from almost every sickness imaginable – diabetes, strokes and a weak heart – and spent much of his life seriously ill before dying very young, aged forty-seven. I loved him very dearly and, as you can imagine, I constantly asked for healing angels to be around him and sent him all the healing grace from me that I could. I know the healing angels helped Joe. One time I found Joe in the garden collapsed (he always tried to do as much as possible around the house and garden irrespective of the state of his health) and he was surrounded by healing angels. I know the healing angels kept him alive longer and kept him more comfortable but, for whatever reason, it wasn't meant to be. Joe and I were not meant to grow old together. He was to go home to Heaven long before me.

We will never know and understand fully why God allows one person to be cured and takes another. I can assure you, though, that healing can happen in many ways. It may not be that the person lives. It may be that the effect of the healing grace that flows to that person from their family means they have less pain, are less stressed or are happier in themselves. Never stop asking the healing angels for help or using the healing grace within you. We think we know what is good for us, what will make us well and happy, but God has a bigger plan.

Many surgeons have told me that they never operate

without asking God for help. Many of them have told me they believe in guardian angels and call on them for help, but I have met very few who are aware of healing angels. However, I believe that no surgeon ever operates without there being healing angels present.

A man told me a beautiful story about his brother, a surgeon in Canada. For a few years the man's brother had been going through a very hard time, had lost his faith in God and had become cynical and bitter. The man told me that his brother had been a brilliant surgeon, but had lost his skill and his confidence. He was in such a dark place that he was fearful of what might happen to him. The man told me he had been so concerned that he eventually went to Canada to visit his brother. The visit didn't help, though. The surgeon just didn't seem to be listening to him and he was considering handing in his resignation and giving up being a surgeon. The man told me that as he was packing his bag to come back to Ireland his brother saw his copy of my first book, *Angels in my Hair*, in his bag. The man had forgotten he had even packed it, and felt that his guardian angel was telling him to give it to his brother.

The man told me that he gave the book to his brother and that his brother had laughed at him, saying he didn't even believe in God, never mind angels. The man made his brother promise that he would read the book, although, to be honest, the man doubted that his brother would do as he said.

After the man came home he kept praying for his brother. The man had been back a few weeks when his brother rang. He told him he had kept his promise and read the book and it had made him think. The surgeon then described how, the day before, an emergency case arose in the hospital and he had been the only surgeon on duty. He was trying to find a tiny fragment of metal in a man's chest, aware that if he didn't find it his patient would die. The patient was bleeding heavily as he tried repeatedly to find what he described to his brother as being like a needle in a haystack. He was about to give up when he got the idea of asking his guardian angel for help. He did so without any real belief or faith that any help would be forthcoming. As he asked, he told his brother, he could feel hands touch his hands, guiding him. He let himself be guided and immediately found the tiny piece of metal and removed it. The patient was now doing well.

The surgeon cried over the phone as he told his brother this, and the man was nearly in tears telling me the story. I know it was his guardian angel's touch that he felt. It is very rare for anyone to feel the guardian angel touching their hands, but in this case I believe it was to give him back confidence in himself and assure him that he had help there. I know there would have been healing angels there that day too.

At most of the public events I do around the world I say the 'Prayer of Thy Healing Angels' that I was given by the Archangel Michael. The prayer – and they are God's words not mine – goes:

Prayer of Thy Healing Angels
That is carried from God by Michael,
Thy Archangel

Pour out, Thy Healing Angels,
Thy Heavenly Host upon me,
And upon·those that I love,
Let me feel the beam of Thy
Healing Angels upon me,
The light of Your Healing Hands.
I will let Thy Healing begin,
Whatever way God grants it,
Amen.

I am hearing from people around the world that they are using this prayer and deriving enormous comfort from it. They are not just using it for healing, but for taking exams or a driving test. I have been told of people saying it when they are out late at night and are in fear of their safety. One farmer told me he says it when he is hoping for rain! I have also been told of people using it as part of a wedding ceremony or funeral.

People often ask about the words, and many people want to correct it to what they consider to be perfect English! I tell them they can't, that these are God's exact words as given to me by the Archangel Michael. The beam of light is the grace of healing that God pours down onto the healing angels so that they can pass it on to us. The prayer refers to the light of God's healing hand.

God gave me this prayer so that it could be spread around the world, so more people could become aware of the healing angels and of the healing that is available to us. This prayer is a gift from God, so why not use it?

CHAPTER SEVEN

A light in the darkness

MOST PEOPLE GET DOWN AND FEEL SAD AND depressed at some time in their lives. If someone is feeling this way, I can recognise it physically within them. It's hard to describe what it is I see. I do see energy around people, what some call an aura, and I have seen this all my life. But it's not here in the aura that I see signs of depression. It's not as if the aura is grey or anything like that. It's within the body that I can see it. It's as if the energy within the body is contaminated in some way, lacking the normal vibrancy. It is completely different to what I see when someone is tired. This is on a deeper level; it's as if the person's eyes are blinded to seeing the light that is around them.

I see this to different degrees, in about one in ten people, perhaps more in these difficult and challenging times, and it affects all ages. But I don't believe that it is with someone for ever. It's something that comes and goes in everyone's life. Some people unfortunately seem to be more prone to it.

One of my son Christopher's friends, Sarah, came to talk to me a few years ago. She had just finished her studies and was starting off in her working life, and over a cup of tea in the kitchen she told me she felt so sad and down. She didn't need to tell me, I could see within her body that something was wrong. She was lacking the vibrancy I see within people who are content.

She told me she was very afraid about what the future held. I could see she seriously lacked courage and confidence. As we talked, her guardian angel opened up and stayed open longer than a guardian angel usually does. It gave a male appearance and was tall and slender with below-shoulder-length, light brown hair. I saw no wings. This guardian angel's face showed unusually strong features. His eyes were deep brown and full of light, and he had such a beautiful smile of love and compassion as he looked down at the young woman. The guardian angel had something in front of him; it wasn't a shield but that's the nearest description I can give. I have no idea what it was there for. His arms were by his side initially and then he moved them up slowly with great gentleness so that his hands were almost, but not quite, holding her shoulders to give her support.

Sarah's guardian angel spoke two words to me silently. To be honest, I can't remember exactly what they were but I knew from them that her guardian angel had some help in hand for her.

As Sarah talked more about how tough she was finding life, her guardian angel went back to being a beam of light behind her. Before she got up to leave, I saw another light appear in front of her, a tiny but bright light. I saw no angel holding the light, but I know there will have been one there, that her guardian angel had invited an angel to hold a light in front of her to give her hope. It was a sign for me that Sarah would get out of this place of darkness and into the light.

I met Sarah a few years later, by accident, on the street. She was so happy and confident and, despite being in her early twenties, was jittery with excitement – like a young teenager. 'Lorna,' she told me, 'I thought I'd never get out of that, that I'd never be happy.' She told me how good life was and that she was aware now that help was there if she suffered from depression in the future.

I believe there are two types of depression. They look different to me when I see it physically in someone's body. By far the most common is a temporary darkness, like Sarah's, which may be to do with events, life phase or even hormones. Most people go through this at some time of their life. Then there is a different type of depression, a depression that is an illness.

Both are extremely painful and difficult to go through, but I believe most people who feel down should not label themselves as being ill. Medication can help some people, but for most people it's not a long-term solution.

Let me share with you first what the angels have told me about what people who are feeling down or depressed can do to help themselves, and then talk about what the angels have told me that the rest of us can do to help.

If you are feeling down or depressed, ask your guardian angel to give you the courage and strength within yourself to get up and do the ordinary things of life, no matter how small they might be: walking to the shop, making a phone call, going out and meeting friends. No one else can get you out of this darkness. You have to do it for yourself. I know some people who are feeling depressed now will find this hard. It is hard, but remember, your guardian angel can help to give you the faith to believe that you can get out of this, that there is light at the end of the tunnel. The angels will work very hard to try and ensure that people around you will help too.

The angels have always told me that everyone must continually remind themselves to see the bright points in their everyday life, however small they might seem. Choose to enjoy the little things, to appreciate the cup of tea you are drinking, the flowers in the garden and a smile on a child's face. When someone is down they get out of the habit of appreciating these things, so you need to constantly remind yourself to enjoy the moment, whatever you are doing.

Angels are great believers in humour. Angels often try and make me laugh, and I see them doing this around people who are out of sorts. Look for opportunities for laughter. Seeing the humour in things can lighten your mood considerably. Even allowing yourself to laugh at a funny movie can be a tonic.

As I write this chapter I'm a bit down myself because of things that are going on in my life and the angels have been trying to get me to lighten up a bit. Yesterday, as I was walking down to the shops, about half a dozen angels ran past me calling out to me to smile. I told them I couldn't smile. They slowed down and stayed in front of me as I walked, joking around with each other like ten-year-olds might have done until eventually they got me to smile. I found it very hard to do, though. I couldn't face going into the little tea-room that I normally go into, in case someone said hello. In a sense I was trying to shut myself away. The angels didn't leave me alone though; they were determined to cheer me up. As I queued at the counter the woman serving the food gave me a big smile. If the woman's smile was big, the smiles of the angels standing on either side of her were enormous. I sat down at a table, avoiding everyone. As I was waiting for my food I decided to distract myself by looking at a newspaper. I went to pick up a paper on a table nearby. As I reached the table there was an angel sitting there reading the paper. 'This is my paper, Lorna,' she said to me.

'No, it's mine!' I replied and despite myself I had to smile. The angel came back with me to the table and sat opposite me, telling me to enjoy the moment. To be honest, in my sad mood I hadn't even been conscious of the delicious food I was eating.

Walking home, I was still feeling very down but

the angels hadn't given up. I could see an elderly man walking towards me, surrounded by angels. As I got closer to him I said to the angels, 'That's George!' George is an elderly man I have known for years. He had been very kind to the children as they were growing up and had known my husband Joe too. I had never met him on this particular road.

'What a coincidence, meeting you, Lorna,' he exclaimed. I had to laugh, knowing it was no coincidence; this was all the angels' work. The angels around him started acting as if they were at a party, mimicking people having a good time. 'It's my birthday today, Lorna. I'm eighty,' George announced and invited me to a party that night to celebrate. I wished him a happy birthday, but said I couldn't go to the party. George didn't take no for an answer though. 'Who knows, you might change your mind,' he said. I know that the angels were whispering to him to leave the door open for me to say yes.

I'm not perfect; I don't always listen to the angels or do what I should do. Sometimes I don't practise what I preach. I didn't go. I felt too down in myself. I know I should have made the effort to go and enjoy myself a little, even for a short time, but I didn't. I rejected an offer of help from George.

*　　*　　*

Try and be aware of people offering help or support. It might be a smile, a sweet left on your desk or an invitation out. People will offer support but sometimes when someone is down they find it hard to see the help that is being offered to them. You can get into a habit of pushing things away from you, of automatically rejecting suggestions or ideas. (As I did with the invitation to George's birthday party.) It can require an effort on your part to smile when you are down or to accept an invitation for a coffee – but you need to make this effort. The angels keep telling me that the only person who can get you out of it is you.

We can be a light, however briefly, in someone else's life.

Being depressed can become a habit. If you notice this tendency within yourself, say *I'm not going to allow this to be a habit* and ask your guardian angel for help. This is particularly true of people who have been grieving. Time to grieve is important but there comes a time when it is important to start to smile and see little joys in life again. This doesn't mean that you are forgetting the person who has died. They are in Heaven, regardless of the circumstances of their death, and they want you to begin to enjoy life again.

Remember, your guardian angel will help in many ways, including calling in the help of other angels. Many people I have met who are depressed have talked about a loved one who was good at enjoying life, or who would have understood how they felt, and I tell them to ask their guardian angel to let the soul of this loved one be around them in order to help.

Your guardian angel is the gatekeeper of your soul, and it can allow a soul who is in Heaven to come back and be with you and give you support and help when you need it. Often it is easier for us to feel the presence and hear the promptings of a loved one than of any angel. These souls, after all, once lived on this earth.

Recognise you are not the only one – you are not alone. Lots of people suffer from feeling down at some time in their lives. There may be people around you today who are feeling more depressed than you. Talking with people about what is going on with you and about what you feel can be a big help. Talk with friends, family, a support organisation, a counsellor or a medical practitioner. Talking about what you are feeling will make you more aware and hopefully will also bring in offers of help and support.

The angels taught me as a child to try and not take things personally. This was important for me, given all the comments that were made about me being retarded, and the way many people treated me as if I was incapable or stupid. The angels told me that these hurtful things said more about the person making the comment than about me. When we are down we are vulnerable, and particularly prone to taking things personally. I know it's hard. I find it hard too, but try and take things less personally.

Prayer is powerful in every circumstance, and it can be a very big help when someone feels depressed. The angels have given me a prayer I use when I am down:

A Prayer for Joy in My Life

Please God,
Take this cloud of darkness away.
Shine your light upon me.
Send your angels to help me.
Give me the courage and strength
To start to feel the joy in my life again.
Amen.

We all need to be aware of how people around us feel, particularly when they are down. I hate the phrase 'Pull yourself out of it.' That implies that it's simple! It's not simple at all for someone who is feeling down to have the courage and strength to 'pull themselves out of it'. If it was that simple, no one would stay down for long. We all need to have compassion and understanding for a person who is down in themselves.

It's not always easy. We need to have lots of patience around people who are feeling low. We should not give up on anyone, but need to keep on offering them support. If someone who is depressed has said no to an invitation ten times, don't give up, ask again, and keep the door open. One of these days they might say yes and that step could be so important to them.

If you know that someone is down, make an effort to help. The little things count: a smile, making that phone call, inviting someone for a cup of tea, dropping in to say hello, having the patience to stop and have a chat. Little acts of kindness help people to recognise the good things that are within their lives. We all benefit from acts of kindness – both the doer and the recipient. Your smile or few words to someone in a queue – someone you may never have met before – might make all the difference to them.

I was with my daughter Ruth in the centre of Dublin one day. Ruth's car was parked in a multi-storey car park and as we queued up at the pay machine the angels whispered to me to pay attention. There were about a dozen people in the queue so I looked at them all. Very quickly I spotted a woman in her late thirties and I could see she was really down. Her body lacked the normal vibrancy. She was at the head of the queue and was searching in her bag for coins. She searched, but didn't seem to find any. She took a credit card out of her bag, and put it away when she realised this particular machine didn't take cards. Behind her in the queue was a smartly dressed, tall, broad man of about sixty. An angel suddenly appeared beside him on his left. The angel was very big and stooped over the tall man, giving a strongly male appearance. I saw no wings. The angel started to whisper to him. He moved a few steps forward to the woman with a hand outstretched, saying, 'Don't worry; here's the change you need.' Her face lit up and her eyes got bigger. She was startled by the kindness of this stranger. And I could see the vibrancy in her body increase dramatically. I have no idea how much it was, probably a few euros. It wasn't about the money. It was the kindness this man was showing to her. She thanked him, and he smiled back, saying, 'It's my pleasure.'

As I stood there waiting for my turn, after both the man and woman had gone the angels told me that this act of kindness was not intended to benefit just the woman who couldn't pay – it was intended also as an example for everyone there in the queue to take heed, and notice an act of kindness being performed. Seeing and taking note of an act of kindness helps open us to other opportunities where we can help others, where we can be a light, however briefly, in someone else's life.

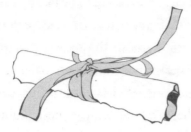

CHAPTER EIGHT

You are meant to live life to the full and enjoy it!

I WAS IN A RESTAURANT IN KILKENNY. IT'S A LONG narrow restaurant and one of the reasons I like it is that from almost every table you can see out of the window onto one of the main streets. I was sitting enjoying a cup of tea when an angel told me to look up. I saw a mother and her daughter of about sixteen, in school uniform, walk into the restaurant and sit down at a table opposite mine. The mother was facing me and the daughter had her back to me. On the right hand side of the mother stood a beautiful angel. I could see long and slender wings, which disappeared into the ceiling. They were like silk, moving slightly, shimmering. The angel was dressed in flowing robes of a light mauve colour, but gave no impression of being either male or female.

I could hear some of the conversation. The daughter was sipping hot chocolate and telling her mum about what was happening in school, and about one of her friends. Several times I overheard the girl say, 'You're not listening, Mum.'

I could see the young girl's frustration with her mother. The mother drank nothing and every so often I would see her look at her watch. I could see the back of the girl and on each side of her was a big angel. At times they would turn and face me. Both angels were tall and elegant and gave a female appearance. I could see no wings. They looked different to one another but were dressed in similar clothes of green. Both angels had a hand on the girl's shoulders, and one angel put her second hand in front of the girl's heart. At times one angel would whisper in her ear. The angels were comforting the teenager, and encouraging her to share what was going on with her mother.

The beautiful angel to the right of the mother was leaning down beside her, whispering into her ear at the same time. The mother still looked preoccupied, fidgeting as if she couldn't wait to leave the restaurant.

Every now and then the angel would look up at me, and it told me without words that this mother believed she didn't have time to listen to her daughter. She thought she was too busy, but in fact there was nothing more important she could be doing at this time. The angel persisted with the mother, though. And her daughter kept talking, encouraged by the angels on either side of her.

Suddenly, the mother's angel stood upright and smiled at me. The mother called the waiter over and ordered tea and a cake. It was as if the mother had forgotten about all the things she had to do and had started to listen to her daughter for the first time. As I watched, the angel remained upright beside her.

The two angels on either side of the girl remained with their hands on her shoulders and every now and then these two beautiful angels resumed whispering to the young girl. As I stood up to leave I heard the mother and daughter laughing. I have no idea how long they stayed there talking but I do hope that the mother will continue to appreciate that it is important to live every moment of life fully – and that time spent with her daughter is very precious, and more important than most of the other things she feels she should be doing.

* * *

The angels that are with me every day tell me that so many of us have got our priorities wrong. We think that our life should be all about doing things, being busy and being successful. Many of us place a lot of importance on money and material things. Having some money is of course important but many of us have placed too much emphasis on it. The angels keep telling me to remind you that when you die you can bring no money or material things to Heaven with you. What you do bring with you are your memories and all the love you felt on this earth. At times we are so busy that we forget to live life and enjoy the ordinary everyday pleasures. We try to cram so much into our busy lives that we actually forget what is important.

I often see angels trying to help people to slow down so that they can enjoy life more. Last week, I watched a man in his forties, wearing a suit and carrying a briefcase, hurrying towards the railway station. There was an angel in front of him with both hands on his chest pushing back against him, as if to slow him down. Every time the man took a step it was like a jolt to the angel, and it worked like brakes to slow the man down. The angel spoke to me without words and told me that the man thought he needed to do everything that day and that he was completely overwhelmed. The angel told me that he had plenty of time to catch his train, so he should be walking slowly and enjoying the fresh air and the sun on his face. The angel had such compassion and love for the man.

A few days later, driving along, I was shown the same man. This time the angels had adopted a different approach to make him slow down. They had him wearing what was like a child's halter, reins you use to stop a toddler from running away; there were two angels pulling on the halter, pulling him backwards, helping him to slow down. The angels were working very hard with this man but I don't know if they will succeed in slowing him down. They do sometimes succeed, though. I was in a shopping centre recently with my daughter Ruth and there was a man sitting on the ledge at the foot of a pillar, surrounded by angels. The man, also in a business suit, was taking time out to enjoy an ice cream and he looked as if he hadn't a care in the world. The angels around him told me he had been very busy, but they had tempted him with the idea of an ice cream and had got him to take some time out – even if only a little – and just sit there living and enjoying life. The angels were helping him to rediscover what he would have known as a child, what every child knows: how to feel fully alive.

Many elderly people tell me that one of the few regrets that they have is that they rushed around too much when they were younger and that it's only now they are learning to enjoy their lives.

I was visiting an elderly neighbour, Mrs Stacey, recently. She was sitting in a big old-fashioned armchair as we chatted. She told me that the previous day she had been out doing her garden and that although she couldn't do much, what she could do she really enjoyed. She told me that she knew her guardian angel was there, giving her a helping hand. As she talked about the joy she had got out of her gardening two angels appeared, sitting on either side of her. It was as if they were sitting on the arms of the chair. The angels looked like spring. One of them had a simple white daisy in its hands and the other one seemed to have flowers of different sorts and different colours scattered in its lap. These all seemed to be bigger and more abundant versions of flowers that we know – among them were pansies and more daisies. It was spring and I knew Mrs Stacey's garden wasn't yet in bloom, but I knew that in summer it would be. The angels were there, helping her to learn to enjoy life to the full. We sat there as she told me that she enjoys life so much more now – that she does her best to get pleasure out of all the simple things she might have ignored or taken for granted in the past. She told me how much less important material things seemed to her now. She did admit, though, that she loved both her big armchair and her garden. She told me that when I left she would go for a walk – a short walk as that is all her body would allow now – but that she would enjoy it and she would stop and talk to anyone who crossed her path during the course of the walk.

The greater part of our lives is made up of all the small things – the ordinary and the everyday. If we ignore these things or dismiss them as trivial and unimportant we will miss out on life. We will miss out on what is really important. Whether we realise it or not, the big things are made up of a lot of little things.

I've said elsewhere that I hate the question, 'What is my destiny?' It seems to imply that life is about one or a few big tasks or goals. My understanding from God and the angels is that each and every one of our destinies is to live life to the full. This means living every minute of every day to the full and trying to be aware and conscious of every moment and, where possible, to enjoy them all. Your life is today. It's not yesterday or tomorrow. It's now. This moment.

Life itself is a precious gift from God. God wants you to live this gift fully and God wants you to enjoy it as much as possible. That's one of the reasons God has given you a guardian angel and angels will always help us to enjoy life to the full if we ask them.

I know life is tough sometimes, and enjoying it can seem to be impossible in those moments – but even in the toughest of times there are always moments that we can savour and enjoy.

Many people have commented on what a tough life I've had, but I don't see it that way. I wouldn't change it for the world. Yes, I've been very poor and at times wondered where the next meal for the family would come from or how to pay the electricity bill. Even through all of that I continued to appreciate the small joys of life. I lost my husband Joe young, and for much of our lives together we had to cope with his sicknesses. But every day there were moments – even very short ones – to be enjoyed.

Ask your guardian angel to help you enjoy the everyday things more – the simple things of life. Try and practise enjoying and seeing the beauty in the things that are around you. Practise doing it for a few minutes at a time until you get into the habit of it. Take a walk, for example – it could be in a busy built-up city. Take the time to notice what is around you. There is always beauty around us. We just don't always notice it and we frequently don't think it is important. It's the little bits of beauty around us that help to teach us to appreciate life. Take a look around and I know you will see something of beauty. It may be a bird, a plant in a pot, a building, a child with a smile or something in a window. There is always something of beauty around us.

In seeing beauty around you, you will appreciate life more, and recognise more the beauty that is within yourself. Appreciating beauty helps you to slow down, and the more beauty you notice, the more beauty you will see. Much of the time we just don't notice what is around us. We are lost in our thoughts or fail to give any importance or value to the idea of seeing beauty. Recognising the beauty around us also helps us to care for our environment.

> **Your life is today. It's not yesterday or tomorrow. It's now. This moment.**

The most important things in our lives are our relationships – from those simple ones with people we pass once in our lives and smile at on a street, to our more in-depth relationships with our families, friends and loved ones. Relationships are priceless. They are much more important than material things, and far too often we take them for granted.

Sitting in the lobby of the Westbury Hotel in Dublin, waiting for a journalist, a well-dressed businessman came up and asked for five minutes of my time. He told me he was wealthy and successful but that he worked extremely hard. He told me he travelled a lot and read a lot on planes. He kept seeing *Angels in my Hair* but the word angels in the title had put him off. He told me that he kept seeing the book – that in every bookshop he went into he saw it. He used to laugh to himself about how he kept seeing it but he was certain the book was definitely not for him. Some months later, he was queuing in a bookshop to pay for books and right in front of him was a pile of copies of *Angels in my Hair*. Finally, he picked it up, thinking he would give it to his wife. He paid and returned with the books to his car.

He put the books on the passenger seat of the car and turned the key in the engine. It wouldn't start. He tried a few times but to no avail. He decided he'd wait a few minutes before trying again. He reached out to pick a book up, not intending to pick up *Angels in my Hair* but he did. He opened the book and started to read. Time passed. He could hardly put the book down. He read for a good half an hour. Eventually, he tried the key again and this time the engine started. He drove home. He couldn't get the book off his mind. What he had read had touched him deeply. He told me he hid the book in the glove compartment of the car so no one could see it and take it from him. He wanted to finish it as soon as possible and the next day he did so.

He said that reading the book shocked him to his core, and made him realise that all his life he had been concentrating on the wrong things. He told me he couldn't remember the last time he'd shown his wife affection, let alone told her he loved her. He had two sons. His younger was in his final year in school and the other was already in college. He told me he never had time for them, that he was always too busy working, making money to acquire material things. He told me that he had never kicked a football with his sons and that he didn't really know them.

His fear was that perhaps it was too late! He told me that after reading the book he prayed every day, begging God and the angels not to allow it to be too late. He told me he didn't want to lose his wife and children. He said that for the first time in his life he realised material things were not the most important things in life.

A week after reading *Angels in my Hair* he went away on an international business trip. He said he was very conscious that he was saying goodbye to his wife and children. He told me he wanted then to open his heart and tell them that he loved them, but he didn't know how and he lacked the courage to do so. When he arrived at his destination he opened his case and in it he found a letter. He sat on the bed looking at the letter in fear. He didn't know what to expect. The first thought that crossed his mind was that it was from his wife, asking for a divorce. He sat there holding the letter in his hand unopened, praying, 'Please God, give me another chance.'

He took a deep breath and opened the letter. It was from his younger son, telling him how much he loved him and wishing that he didn't have to travel so much. The father was stunned. As he said to me, 'This was the first miracle – or at least the first one that I recognised.' His son had never done anything like this before. He said he couldn't wait to get home and tell his wife and sons that he loved them, and that's exactly what he did.

'We are a real family now,' he said. 'Your message

has changed my life and that of my family so much. I appreciate so much more now the ordinary, everyday things of life. To be honest, you have probably saved my life.'

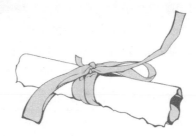

CHAPTER NINE

Angels help the financially stressed

Two unemployed angels stepped out of the queue at a book-signing and waved at me to get my attention. The angels stood beside a man in his early thirties and connected me with the man so that I could feel his emotions. I could feel considerable fear and anxiety that filled me with dread as I talked with others ahead of him in the queue. After about twenty minutes he got to the head of the queue and came and sat down. He told me he had been unemployed for some months.

'Lorna,' he said, 'if I don't get a job soon, I won't

be able to support my wife and little daughter. We are going to be like beggars.' There were tears rolling down his face as he talked.

A very tall angel appeared beside him. Initially I thought it was female but it seemed to switch every few seconds from male to female. It was a golden colour – so bright – and glowed like the sun. The angel spoke to me without words, 'Lorna, you have to give him hope and courage.'

My heart felt really heavy; the man was so upset and I felt so helpless. I said to the angel, 'But how can I give him hope? I can't give him a job.'

The angel replied, 'Tell him we will help.'

At this moment, I moved my hands forward and the man caught my hand. The angel lit him up – a beautiful gold colour. I know it was to fill him with hope. I listened to the angel: 'Every job opportunity that comes to his attention he is to go for. He shouldn't think too hard about whether it's a job he wants to do or not, he should just apply. He should remember that the first job will just be a stepping stone to another one.'

I repeated what the angel had said to the man. The angel continued, 'Tell him there is no loss of dignity in asking others for help. Everyone needs help at some time in their lives and in future he will be called upon to help others. Tell him he is not to give up, we will bring his attention to jobs and he will have to keep applying.'

I know that the hope the angels' message gave him provided enormous comfort. He left the signing with the strength and confidence to apply for those jobs. I asked the angels as he left whether he would be successful and they answered, 'Yes, as long as he plays his part and listens to us.' I said a prayer as he left that he would listen to the angels.

I meet and hear from so many people all around the world who are worried about money these days, worried about meeting their own and their family's basic needs. I understand very well how stressful this is. I myself suffered poverty at different times in my life. As a five-year-old, my four brothers and sisters, my parents and I were left homeless after the old cottage we were living in, in Old Kilmainham in Dublin, collapsed. Then we had to live with a relation for several years, before getting a council house.

My husband Joe was sick and unable to work for much of our marriage, and things were very tight financially. I have told the story elsewhere that we were only able to have food on one particular Christmas Day due to the kindness of a stranger who put money into an envelope and dropped it through the letterbox on Christmas Eve.

I know the angels can and do help to make things easier for us when we are under financial pressure; they did it for me and my family and I see them helping people every day. Of course, I do understand people who have their doubts about this, who feel that their problems are too big to be helped by angels, that if there really was a powerful guardian angel beside them, minding them, they wouldn't have these financial problems.

I keep saying that God and the angels didn't cause the economic problems that we have in many countries now – people did. Many people stopped listening to God and the angels. Instead, they decided that money and material possessions were the most important things in life. Everyone needs enough money to live, but some people had become too greedy. The angels didn't cause these economic problems, but they can help us out of them. They are a gift from God and they want to help us; it's such a shame not to make use of this help.

I sometimes walk past the local social welfare office, where people who are unemployed are given financial assistance. Unfortunately, recently the queue has often stretched out the door. As I walk past, I see angels, in addition to the guardian angels with each and every person there.

> **The angels will do their best to help you financially but you have to play your part too.**

One day, the angels brought my attention to a young man who was standing in the queue with a pile of papers in his hand. There were three unemployed angels there with him. One of them was continually whispering to him. Another talked to me without words and told me that he was feeling shocked and hopeless. He had just become unemployed and was going to apply for social assistance for the first time. The angel told me that they had been prompting him over the past few days to make sure that he would remember to bring all the correct papers with him, so he would be able to sign on without any delay. They were also whispering to him to ask the right questions when he eventually got to the head of the queue. The angels were telling him he was to ask about training schemes he might be eligible for. The angels were working hard to keep his spirits up, to give him hope for the future so that he would make the best of any opportunities that were there for him.

Of course, it's not only people and families who are unemployed who are struggling at the moment; lots of people with jobs are struggling to make ends meet or to pay off debts.

Many people have tightened their belts – some quite severely. And I see angels helping with this in all kinds of simple and some might say ordinary ways. But our lives are made up of simple ordinary things.

It's the school holidays. Yesterday, I took a break from working on this book by walking to a local café. There was a mother there with her three children and I watched as they queued up to order. The angels were working hard, playing with the children and keeping them entertained. There was an angel with the mother and she told me that the woman was really worried about money, but that she was determined that the children would enjoy their holidays. She bought a coffee for herself and orange squash for the children. She also bought one cream slice.

I watched as she sat down and cut the cream slice in three so that each of the children could have a piece. She had none herself. I watched the angels with the children; they were making 'mmm . . . delicious' sounds, licking their lips and reminding the children how delicious the cream slice they were eating was.

The children were happy and the mother gave a sigh of relief that they weren't looking for a cream slice each, or fighting with each other.

It was a small thing, but I see angels helping us in this way all the time, helping us to enjoy our life in spite of any financial concerns we might feel. The angels also show me people who are generating unnecessary financial stress for themselves.

Someone asked me to meet a couple in need of help. I met them in a local hotel and as I arrived in the lounge they were sitting in a corner surrounded by unemployed angels. The man had sheets of paper in front of him and almost immediately after I had sat down, they started telling me of their financial problems. He listed their monthly outgoings and she added more for good measure. The angel beside him told me to make them stop. I did get them to, with difficulty. I asked them a little about themselves. The man, who was in his early forties, had a good and stable job and she worked every morning, close to where they lived. They had three children, one in senior school and two in primary school.

The angel beside her said, 'They are working out their money the wrong way. Many of their expenses are unnecessary.' That angel told me to ask them again about their monthly expenses. I did so and, as the husband talked, the angel told me that I was to suggest three things to them.

I asked as gently as I could whether all their expenses were necessary. I did as the angel asked and suggested that they mightn't really need a second car as the wife worked locally, that the children didn't need to be doing *all* those extra activities and that they might be able to eat out less often.

The man threw his hands up, protesting, 'I can't cut back on the things the children need.'

The angel beside him said, 'It's really sad. They treat the family's finances as if it's a business. They are getting very little enjoyment at all out of their family life and are putting themselves under so much unnecessary pressure.'

I talked with the couple for about another fifteen minutes. I know I didn't say what they wanted to hear – they wanted to hear how the angels were going to help them to increase their income, so that they could maintain their lifestyle. But eventually they did listen to me.

I heard nothing from them afterwards – no thanks, no nothing. I feared the angels' advice had fallen on deaf ears. About a year later, I got a text from them, thanking me and saying that they had cut back and that their lives were going well. The angels will do their best to help you financially but you have to play your part too. Hard as this may be for some to hear, angels are not here to help us to win the lottery! You must take the steps – whatever they are – to help yourself. The angels will prompt you but it's up to you to listen and act.

We are all called upon to help people who are feeling financially stressed. We can give encouragement or advice. No matter how financially stressed we may feel there are always people who are worse off and we need to help.

I was in a restaurant recently when a young girl came in looking for work. There was an angel with her. When the boss of the restaurant came out to talk to her there were two angels with him. As he talked with the girl the angels whispered to him. The angel with the girl told me that this man could and should give the girl part-time work, and this is what the angels were whispering to him about. He didn't listen, though, and the girl left without a job.

Of course, all of our individual finances are tied up as part of a much bigger picture. The angels assure me that they are working hard with local, national and international leaders to improve the economy globally – to improve economic conditions for everyone but particularly those in need. We need to pray that our leaders listen to God and the angels.

I know some people will find it frustrating if I say that prayer can help to reduce financial stress. But I know it can. I asked the Angel Amen to give me a prayer that people who are feeling hopeless because of their financial situation can say. Here is the prayer:

A Prayer for Hard Times

God,
Pour the grace of hope upon me and allow
me always to see the light of hope
burning brightly in front of me.
Light up the darkness by filling me with
faith and hope and allowing me to receive
the comfort of your love.
Give me the courage and strength to know
that I will get through these hard times.
Fill me with the joy and trust of knowing
that I am your child and that you will
care for me and those I love.
Hear my prayer.
Amen.

CHAPTER TEN

No one dies alone

I MEET MANY PEOPLE WHO TELL ME THEY ARE fearful of dying. I will often tell them that if God would take me today, I would go gladly, hard as that might be to explain to my children, who are still very young!

A young woman with two little children came up to me one morning in Connolly railway station in Dublin. She explained that her grandfather had been very ill and was afraid of dying. Her brother brought a copy of my first book, *Angels in my Hair*, into the hospital and each day different members of the family used to sit by the grandfather's bed and read it aloud to him. Sometimes he would appear to go to sleep as they read and they would stop, and then he would open an eye from the bed and say, 'Keep going.' Reading the book once wasn't enough for him. The book was read aloud to him from cover to cover again and again. She had no idea how many times it was read in the weeks that he was dying. In this way all the family got to understand more about angels and understand that death wasn't the end. According to her, it had a profound effect on everyone. They became kinder and more optimistic; they were more patient and loving around everyone – not just their dying grandfather.

She told me that when they were about a quarter of the way through the second reading of the book, her grandfather had said that he had got the message he was waiting for. That he was not afraid to die any more. He appeared to lose his fear and become much happier in himself; he also seemed to have less pain, which was a tremendous relief to him and to all his family. He died peacefully a week or so later.

A few years after Joe died I had major surgery lasting six or seven hours. The angels had told me before the surgery that I might have a little problem, but that I would recover. Lying on the stretcher going into theatre, the angels were standing around the surgeon and they told me he was the best surgeon possible. Again, they mentioned I would be fine but there might be a little problem. Their definition of a little problem and mine were somewhat different!

The surgery went fine. I remember an angel walking beside me, holding my hand, as I was pushed out of surgery. I was put into a post-operative recovery room some distance away from the nurses rather than in one that had constant supervision.

The surgeon told me afterwards that they only heard the alarms by my bed going off because the door was inexplicably ajar. I had stopped breathing and the medical team were sure they had lost me. I was on a very wide bright stairway that curved upwards. An angel was holding my hand and telling me to hurry. I was very happy and could feel nothing of my human body. I was full of joy; I knew where I was going – to Heaven – and I was so happy to be going there. I had no sadness or thoughts of leaving my children behind me. There were hundreds of souls with me on their way to Heaven. With each of them was their guardian angel. In some cases the guardian angel was walking beside them. Others were holding their hand and in a few cases, the guardian angels

– who were enormous – were carrying the souls in their arms with great tenderness, a bit like carrying a baby. The look on each guardian angel's face was one of pure love. Around each soul there were also hundreds of other angels.

I was fascinated, watching the souls on their way to Heaven; they were happy, completely at peace, there were no tears, no sign of stress. It was as if in some way the souls were in a queue to go to Heaven. Other souls came down to greet them and they seemed to talk in a human way with great excitement. I could tell the difference between the souls that hadn't yet reached Heaven and those that were greeting them. The souls that had been in Heaven for a while were much more radiant, much brighter, and their human appearance was less marked than those of the souls who had just left the earthly world.

The angel beside me was telling me to rush, that we had to hurry. We were going much faster than the other souls, overtaking them, but no one seemed to mind. In fact, some of them called out to me and told me to hurry up. I felt wonderful, I felt perfect. I had left my human body and any pain behind. I was going to where I wanted to be and I was so happy. I had no fear or anxiety, I had no thoughts at all of anyone left behind – not even Megan, who was still very young and had already lost a father.

I wasn't allowed to stop and ask questions. I didn't know why I had to move so fast, but it seemed in some way to be natural. The journey seemed to go on for ages, but in other ways it was a very short journey. Time is different in Heaven.

When I got to wherever I was meant to be in Heaven I was suddenly alone, not an angel in sight, although I know my guardian angel was still there. It was as if there was beautiful sand under my bare feet and I could feel the smooth silky warm sand between my toes. The sand was in small hills and I could see a beautiful tree in the distance on top of one of the hills. The tree was big, covered in leaves and looked perfect in every way.

I hadn't a care in the world. It was like being a little child again. I went and sat down under the tree for a little while and then started playing at rolling down the hill. After a short while I heard a voice and knew immediately it was God's.

'Lorna, you must go back,' the voice boomed.

This was my second near-death experience. The first time, I had begged to be allowed to stay in Heaven. This time I didn't protest, as I knew I wouldn't be listened to anyway. An angel took me by the hand – I have no idea which angel it was – and brought me back. I have no memory of coming back into my body.

Some weeks later, the surgeon told me that I had been gone for ten minutes and they hadn't been sure whether they could revive me or not. Some days after the operation I became conscious in intensive care. The surgeon expected me to have brain damage, and was surprised that there were no signs of it.

I know that one of the reasons I have been given these experiences is so that I can share them with all of you. So that I can help you to understand that there is nothing to fear in death.

I know one of the reasons people fear death is that they are concerned about those they will leave behind. At the moment of death you will realise that you can do much more for those you love in Heaven than you can ever do for them on this earth. I know this is hard to understand. When a soul has gone to Heaven it is in a position to intercede with God in a much more powerful way, on behalf of family and loved ones, than it could when it was here on earth.

After you have died you are allowed to be with your family spiritually when they need you. The guardian angels of your family members and loved ones allow your soul to be around your family when they need comfort or encouragement or strength – or simply need to feel that you are OK. You will still be in Heaven but for those few minutes you will also be with your loved ones. In some cases, they will even feel your presence and love and be reassured by it. You may also at times be able to give signs or messages of reassurance, with the help of the angels and other people, to those you loved.

I see souls with people all the time. When a soul comes back to be with a person, what I am shown looks like a person but is glowing and surrounded by a light. It is very clear to me they are a soul not a living person. They may have died and gone to Heaven in their old age but often I will be shown them in their prime.

One day in a café, my attention was drawn to a young girl of about twenty, sitting at a table on her own. She was surrounded by angels and there in the middle of them was the soul of a man. An angel told me he was her father, who had died six months previously. I was allowed to hear him whispering in her ear, 'I'm OK. I love you.' He continued encouragingly: 'I want you to get on with your life. I don't want to see you moping around and I want you to go back to college and get those exams.' The last thing I heard him say before I left the café was, 'I am so proud of you.'

When you die, you won't want to come back, not even for your loved ones. I know that both times I have died and gone to Heaven, I didn't want to come back. I also knew that no matter how much my loved ones might grieve, they still needed to lead their own lives without me.

A comfort for everyone, whether dying or grieving, is the knowledge that you will eventually meet your loved ones again. That you will be reunited when it is their time to come home to Heaven. God and the angels have told me this since I was a very young child – we all will meet our loved ones again. This is something all of us need to hold in our hearts.

I have met many people of all religions whose greatest fear about dying is that God will judge that their lives have not been good enough. I've also met people who say they don't believe in God but are fearful that there may in fact turn out to be a God, and that He might turn them away. I have to say that while God has told me that Hell exists, He has never shown me Him sending any soul to Hell and I hope and pray that He never does. Nor has He shown me any soul being sent to a place because it wasn't yet good enough for Heaven. I have never been shown anything other than a soul going directly to Heaven.

> **At the moment of death you will realise that you can do much more for those you love in Heaven than you can ever do for them on this earth.**

God has endless compassion; to be honest, I don't have the words to express it. He is Our Father and He wants us all home. No matter what we have done, He wants us in Heaven if at all possible.

We should have more compassion for ourselves and others and we should forgive more – both ourselves and others. We should all be willing, throughout our lives, to ask for forgiveness both from God and from people we have wronged. We are only human and we all make mistakes; none of us is perfect.

Equally, we should all be more willing to forgive. To forgive does not mean that you need to forget the wrong that has been done to you, nor that you should not take steps to protect yourself from future hurt. But forgiveness releases you and sets you free. Forgiving ourselves is important. In forgiving yourself you give yourself peace and allow yourself to become more loving to everyone around you. This is important at all times, but particularly when people are near the end of their lives. In forgiving yourself, you forgive everyone around you.

God is very forgiving and all we have to do is ask him for forgiveness. Simply ask using your own words, or here is a little prayer that the angels have given me:

A Prayer for Forgiveness and Peace of Mind

God,
Please forgive me for all my imperfections,
For all the wrong I have done.
Give me the grace to forgive those that have
*   hurt me.*
Amen.

It is never too late to ask for forgiveness, regardless of what you have done. God has infinite mercy. I have sometimes been told that someone died without asking for forgiveness, but we have no idea what they might have done in their last moments; they may have asked for forgiveness.

God and the angels have also asked me to tell you that if you can forgive someone who has wronged you, you can also ask God that He will forgive that person too. God will do this for you, because you yourself have forgiven them and have asked God to forgive them also. This is very powerful and this is the prayer I have been given for this:

A Prayer for Forgiveness of Those Who Have Hurt Me

Dear God,
Please forgive those that have hurt me
* because I forgive them.*
Amen.

Occasionally, someone will tell me of a relative or friend who was alone when they died. No one dies alone. Your guardian angel is there with you holding on to your soul and will bring it safely home to Heaven.

I was walking down a corridor in a hospital in Dublin on one occasion and the angel with me told me to stop and look in the open door to a room. There was a woman in a bed. There was no one with her at all, but she was surrounded by angels. Her guardian angel, who was enormous, was bent over her, lifting her soul up out of her body ever so gently. Her guardian angel radiated gold. It didn't give a male or female appearance but seemed to be dressed in heavy robes – like velvet. The guardian angel was looking at the soul it was holding with such love and tenderness. At the end of the bed there was the soul of a loved one, a woman who was radiant and smiling with her arms outstretched to the woman in the bed. The woman in the bed's soul was halfway out of the body, with her guardian angel gently holding it. The soul was delighted. There was no fear or anxiety. She knew she was going home and was overjoyed. The entire room was bathed in a wonderful golden light.

I stood there watching, knowing that there was no need for me or anyone else to do anything. It was her time and she was going peacefully and joyfully. I said a prayer – not for her, but for those she loved who would miss her.

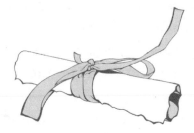

CHAPTER ELEVEN

Angels do play Cupid

I HAVE NEVER SEEN AN ANGEL WITH A BOW AND arrow. But I do see angels helping us in our love lives, so they do play Cupid!

You'd be amazed if you could see just how much angels do to help with romantic love. I see them whispering to people, nudging couples together, arranging circumstances so that people can meet or standing between a couple who are rowing to soften the dispute. I sometimes even see them tying a very fine gold thread of light around a couple to help to bind them together and teach them how to love each other. I also see them trying to lessen the pain when a couple has decided to separate or divorce.

There are lots of different types of love – love for a child, love for a friend, love for nature. I see love as a light that flows from one person to another person or thing, but romantic love looks different to me: it's brighter and more vibrant. Many of us know that this love is different because we have been in love ourselves.

Romantic love is important to all of us, and it's something that most of us search for and want in our lives but it's also one of the most difficult forms of love, largely because of our unrealistic expectations. Nevertheless, the angels want us to have romantic love in our lives and work very hard to help us let it in and keep it alive.

I was walking down a street when the angels around me whispered to me to look ahead. The street was busy with people and angels and then, some distance away, I saw some angels waving to me. There were four angels and they were with four people in their late twenties – two men and two women. The angels told me to walk more slowly. I did so, all the time watching the four people. I asked the angels without words whether there was something wrong. They didn't answer me.

As I got nearer, one man and woman left, leaving what looked like a couple. The four angels stayed with the couple. The angels were trying to get them to stand closer to each other: one angel nudged the man and he took a step closer. At the same time, an angel was whispering to the woman. She wasn't listening, though, and took a step backwards. I was near enough now to overhear their conversation. She was doing most of the talking and seemed to be arguing with him in accented English. My impression was that they were both from Eastern Europe but since they were speaking English I presume they came from different countries.

The woman was tall, taller than the man. The angel beside the man told me that he loved the woman very much, that they were a couple but that he was afraid of losing her. The angel beside the woman completed the story, telling me that while she loved him, she believed he wasn't good enough for her, she felt he wasn't perfect and in particular that he wasn't tall enough or good-looking enough.

The angels told me that this couple were meant to be together and they were doing everything they could to help her to see his good points and to give him the courage and confidence not to give up.

As I reached them, the angels told me to walk closer

to the couple. I passed them on the left-hand side of the woman and, as I did, the beautiful angel with her bent over and turned her head, looking directly into the woman's eyes and face. I could see the light from the angel lighting up her eyes and face, helping her to open her heart and mind and comprehend the love she had for this man and to understand that appearances didn't matter. It was touching to see how hard this angel was working to try and ensure that this woman didn't walk away from this man and their love.

As I continued on walking I said a prayer for the couple. The angels were doing all they could to help the couple to make the right decision but angels can't overstep the boundaries of free will.

A young woman called Sophie told me she had asked her guardian angel to help her to meet her soulmate. She told me that she had gone out with a number of young men but that it never lasted and that she was currently going out with a young man called Anthony. As she spoke, an angel standing beside her spoke to me without words: 'She is being too hard in her judgement of him.'

Sophie told me that Anthony didn't understand her and that he wasn't as intelligent as her. She told me she only wanted to marry her soulmate.

'You have to give him a chance,' I said. 'And yourself a chance, too. No one is perfect, and you are not perfect either.'

She looked a bit startled as she admitted, 'I suppose I'm not.'

'You have got to give each other a chance to learn how to love each other. Ask your guardian angel to allow an angel of love to come and help you and Anthony learn how to love each other. The angel can help you to discover whether you can love each other enough to marry and have a family, or whether you should part.'

 We all have to learn to accept that no one is perfect, including ourselves.

Angels of love are a type of teacher angel; they can teach us how to allow romantic love into our lives and they help us to avoid sabotaging ourselves. They also do a lot to help ensure that we are given the opportunity to meet the right people. They look quite distinctive from other teacher angels. They wear pastel, multicoloured cloaks that fit close to their head and come all the way down to the ground. This cloak is very fine and light but not even a breeze moves it.

Most of us invite angels of love to help in our lives – even unconsciously. Some of us even invited them in as children, through our enjoyment of fairy tales with their 'And they all lived happily ever after' endings.

Never worry about what angel you need to ask for. If you ask your guardian angel for help it will call on the help of the appropriate angel. There is so much help there, so many different types of angels, and your guardian angel knows exactly which angel you need. So just ask your guardian angel.

Some months later, at a book-signing, I met Sophie again. She told me she was going to break up with Anthony that evening. She told me that even though he had told her he loved her and she felt she loved him she didn't feel that their love was strong enough. She didn't think they were soulmates. I could see an angel of love right beside her talking to her, but she wasn't listening. I suggested to her that very few people meet their soulmate, but she was adamant she would.

A few weeks later, I was walking through Dublin window-shopping when an angel told me to look ahead. I looked up a street crowded with people and the light of a guardian angel opened up behind a young woman. I could see what love the guardian angel had for her but the angel said nothing. I walked in the direction of the young woman, who was standing still and texting. When I got closer I recognised it was Sophie.

As I walked towards her, she looked up from her mobile phone and rushed towards me. She immediately started to tell me about her break-up with Anthony. 'I have been such a fool; I have made a terrible mistake, breaking up with Anthony. I never realised how much I loved him and how lonely I'd be without him.' The angel of love right behind her embraced her, comforting her as she was near to tears.

She told me she was to meet Anthony for a drink a few days later and she was hoping that they would get back together again. She asked me to pray for them.

I told her she needed to be very truthful with him and to listen attentively to what he had to say and that I would ask God and the angels to let whatever was best for them happen. I did hear later that the two of them got back together again and are still together.

Very few people marry their soulmates. We all have a soulmate, a soul we met in Heaven before we were born, and with whom we have a deep spiritual connection. I believe we all have only one soulmate but I don't know why God created soulmates. In my whole life I have only met two couples who were soul-mates. I loved my husband Joe, but I know he wasn't my soulmate.

Let me tell you one sad story about soulmates. Some years ago, I met an unmarried man in his seventies. We talked about life and love and he told me he had been very much in love when he was a young man. He showed me an old black-and-white photo of him, looking handsome and dancing with an attractive girl with shoulder-length hair in an old-fashioned ballroom. When he showed me the photo it was as if the angels surrounding him lit up the picture and brought it to life; it was wonderful to see the loving couple dancing together cheek to cheek and I could see the love that was there between them.

He told me that the girl had loved him too, but had rejected his proposal of marriage and married someone else. He told me he had never told anyone the reason she had given for turning him down. There was a genetic illness in his family that meant there was a possibility that any children they had would be disabled. As he told me this story there were three angels around him, consoling and comforting him. He told me he had gone out with other women but that he had never fallen in love in the same way again.

As he talked, I asked one of the angels with him

whether this woman had been his soulmate. The angel nodded. I felt so sad. It seemed such a shame; meeting and falling in love with your soulmate is such an unusual occurrence and it was so sad that she hadn't taken the chance of a life together for better or worse. I couldn't, of course, tell him that she had in fact been his soulmate as that would have completely broken his heart.

Your soulmate may be the same sex as you, born a hundred years apart from you or born on the other side of the world. Your soulmate may be a child with a severe disability who lives only a few years.

If you search only for your soulmate, you may miss love altogether.

Love is precious – but it's not perfect. People aren't perfect. Sophie could have missed out on a happy and fulfilling relationship with Anthony because she wanted him to be perfect. We all have to learn to accept that no one is perfect, including ourselves. Even if you did manage to marry your soulmate, he or she would not be perfect. I have met many women and men in their fifties who tell me that they had loved someone, but because their partner was not perfect in their eyes, they are not together now. They are looking for love, but many of them don't realise that they already had it.

Love is not just about happiness and laughter. Like all of life, it has its ups and downs. I know love hurts; I've experienced this hurt – and so has anyone who has really loved. If it didn't hurt, we wouldn't grow in love. Dealing with the hurt requires strength and compassion, and this can bring people closer together and make their love stronger.

At book-signings I meet men and women of all ages asking me to ask the angels to help them to meet someone to love, perhaps to have a family with. At one particular signing, a man in his thirties asked for this. I sat there and laughed, telling him that at that very signing I had at least ten women, many of whom were his age and very beautiful, looking for the same thing.

I asked, 'Did you say hello or talk to any people in the queue as you were waiting to see me?' He had been waiting about four hours. He told me he was too shy.

People who want to meet partners mustn't let opportunities pass to start a conversation, to get to know someone. Everyone is afraid and nervous, but ask your guardian angel to help you. Regardless of what age you are, it is never too late.

Angels help us to meet people. I see this often. Recently, in a coffee shop I regularly go to, I saw angels working hard to help two students to meet. He was a tall, good-looking young man of about twenty, whom I had noticed several times having coffee on his own. One day, an angel beside him told me he was here hoping to run into a young female student who used to come in sometimes with her friends. A few days later, the angels pointed out a good-looking girl with long, dark hair, chatting with her friends. He was at another table on his own and although he looked over occasionally he did nothing to say hello to her. About a week later, I was in the café again and the young man and the girl and her friends were there too. I watched as an angel with the young man whispered in his ear. I know the angel was helping to give him courage. Eventually, the young man stood up and walked across to the girl and her friends, asking if he could borrow their sugar. At his table, another angel gave me a big smile and signalled to a full sugar bowl. The man had found the courage to come up with an excuse to make contact. As he chatted briefly to the girls at their table I saw an angel whisper into the ear of the girl he liked. She seemed to become rather shy as he talked with them briefly, while the other girls there became rather giddy.

This was a first step, and I know the angels will continue to work to try and bring them together, whispering to them to go to particular places, or to give them courage. If they listen, there is a chance that this relationship could work out – but they will always have free will to make the decision whether to listen or not, and to decide whether to choose this person or not.

When the angels help us to meet someone, it doesn't mean that that person is the love of your life. It may be to teach you how to ask someone out, or how to go on a date, or to bring you into contact with another person with whom you become romantically involved.

There were fire-eaters busking on Dublin's Grafton Street one day as I was walking to an interview, and they were surrounded by a big crowd of people. The angels brought my attention to a couple who were about seventeen years old, holding hands. They were surrounded by angels showing me the love that was between them. The young girl was finding it hard to see and the young man was manoeuvering her through the crowd, putting her in front of him so she could see better. The angels were showing me that he was putting her first. Later on, I saw the same couple again, walking along hand in hand. I had to smile because, this time, it looked as if the angels had wrapped a fine golden light like a thread around both of them at waist height. An angel behind the young man turned and looked at me for a moment and then he whispered into the young man's ear. He let go of his girlfriend's hand and put his arm around her shoulder, pulling her closer to him. As he did so the gold thread around them seemed to become a little tighter, yet it still was quite loose. The angel looked back at me again and spoke to me without words, 'Lorna, this thread of light is to bind the young couple together while they learn about love.'

The fine thread of gold light is something I don't see very often, but it is something the angels of love use to help people, particularly young people, to learn more about love. It binds them together a bit more but it is not forced, it is still kept loose. This way they are more likely to stay together through the ups and downs and learn more about the experience of romantic love. I have seen this fine thread wound around young couples for several weeks, even months. I'm not quite sure why the angels wrap it around one young couple and not another. It seems to be because one or both of the people involved need some extra support and help while they learn about love. I know that it doesn't imply that this couple should be together forever or anything like that.

Occasionally, I will see this fine thread of golden

light around an older couple – as if helping them with lessons of love that they may never have learnt or may have forgotten. Sometimes, with an older couple the angels will tell me that one of them is falling in love for the first time and that this thread is to help to give them courage. No one is ever too old to learn how to love romantically.

I sometimes see angels of love with homosexual couples. Not long ago, I saw angels of love around two young men as they walked down the street. They weren't holding hands or anything like that, but the angels of love with them told me they were partners and very happy. It was lovely to see. Some people find it hard to accept that God and the angels could approve of romantic love between two men or two women. All I can say is that I see angels of love with such couples often.

The angels of love work hard with couples who have been together a long time. Romantic love isn't a bed of roses and it requires a lot of work. We are all human and none of us is perfect. Very few relationships or marriages don't have rocky patches. When a couple are having a difficult time, I see the angels of love wrap a shawl of love around the shoulders of each partner to try and ease the pain and hurt, to try and help them to see their partner's good points, to see what they have together. This shawl is light, like silk, not heavy like a blanket, and it sits easily and lightly on our shoulders.

When one of a couple starts picking a fight, or revisiting old hurts, they try to shrug off this shawl of love, and the angels have to work very hard to keep it wrapped around them. I have known couples where the angels of love have been working constantly for years on keeping the peace. I see them continually wrapping a shawl of love around both of the couple's shoulders

Most couples who meet and fall in love believe that they should grow old together, but sometimes that is not the case. Sometimes, love for the other dies in one of them. Sometimes, love only lasts a short time. Hard as it may be to understand, the angels tell me that some couples are not supposed to be together for life. But romantic love is a very special and precious thing, and for however long it lasts it should be appreciated.

Sometimes a person makes a mistake and realises years into a relationship that the partnership is wrong, that they don't love the person they are with enough to share their life with them. The love within this person has died and leads to separation, even though the other person in the couple may still have great love. This happens because we are only human and it is very sad and very hard for everyone involved.

I have asked God and the angels why all marriages cannot be made in Heaven, but I have been given no answer. I have been told, though, that when marriages are made in Heaven the only way they will separate is when one of the couple goes back home to Heaven.

Love is precious and even if you only have it for a very short time it is wonderful. The angels tell me that when a couple breaks up the best thing is to remember that love and not to let too much bitterness and hate come in. I know this is incredibly hard to do. Ask your guardian angel for help.

I met a woman who told me she had been going through a horrible divorce – very bitter and stressful. I suggested she ask her guardian angel for help and to ask it to ask the guardian angel of her husband. When she met me some months later she told me it hadn't changed the fact that she and her husband were divorcing, or the difficulties over home and money, but that there was a big change. 'We can now sit in the room and discuss things, and we don't seem to be trying to hurt each other every time we talk.' She asked me to thank God and the angels for making things easier.

People sometimes get mixed up and think that the

children have to get caught up in the divorce. A divorce should not be about the children. It's about the couple. I know parents who use the children as weapons against each other. They do it because the loss of love is hurting them so much. They don't mean to hurt their children, but they do. It is completely wrong to drag your children into the crossfire – tempting as it may seem. Ask your guardian angel to help you not to do this. Remember that your children (whatever age they may be) were little souls in Heaven before they were born and chose both of you as their parents – knowing that there could be a separation or divorce.

Many of us get into a rut in a relationship. We take the love for granted, get caught up in our day-to-day living and forget to fan the fire of romantic love. You need to consciously keep the light of love burning within you. The little gestures matter! So remember to pay compliments, to buy the odd bunch of flowers, to take the time out with a special dinner to celebrate. Your love is very precious. Again, ask your guardian angel to let in the angels of love to help you.

I see the angels prompting couples – particularly couples who are not in their early years of love – to make romantic gestures all the time. I was walking across the park at Kilkenny Castle and there was a middle-aged couple sitting on bench. They were sitting apart and weren't talking. An angel with the woman told me that she was feeling unloved and taken for granted. I watched as an angel of love whispered to the man. He did nothing for a few minutes but then I watched him stand up. I was afraid to watch too closely in case they saw me watching them. But I looked back a few minutes later to see him presenting her with a little bunch of daisies he had picked from the grass. Her face lit up with pleasure. The angels will help us to bring romance into our lives – all we have to do is ask, listen and then act on what we are told.

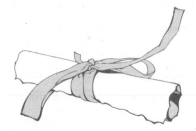

CHAPTER TWELVE

You are more than any angel

I SEE ANGELS PHYSICALLY EVERY DAY, AND THEY
are very beautiful. But you have a soul, which is much
more beautiful than any angel. Each and every one
of us human beings, regardless of religion or beliefs,
is God's child. God loved us all so much that He gave
us each a little spark of Himself. This speck of the
light of God is our soul.

On occasions, I have been privileged to be allowed
to see a human soul. When I see someone's soul it
takes my breath away because souls are unbelievably
beautiful. To be honest, I think they are probably

indescribable and I am still searching for words to describe this beauty.

> **Because we have souls that are in the image of God we are more than any angel.**

About a year ago I was visiting my mother, who lives on her own in the country. She's now in her mid-eighties. She has learnt a lot more about me since I started talking about what I have been seeing all my life and I was thrilled when she came to the launch of my first book.

On this day we had gone out to do some shopping, had had some lunch and were back sitting and chatting in Mum's front room. Later, I went into the kitchen to make tea when Angel Hosus knocked on the window and came in and joined me. 'God wants to show you something very special,' he said. 'Go and have a look in the front room.' I walked quietly down to the door of the front room, which was ajar, and peeped in. My mother was fast asleep in the chair by the fire. 'She looks so peaceful sleeping there,' I said to Angel Hosus without words. He told me to keep watching. As I stood there looking at my mother and thinking how much I loved her, I got a big surprise.

The light of her guardian angel grew extremely

bright. At the same time, my mother's soul sat up out of her body. My mother's soul glowed so, so brightly – it was many times brighter than her guardian angel, or any angel. The light of a soul is perfect and crystal clear; no light in the world can resemble the light of a soul in any way, not even the light of the biggest, brightest diamond, because the soul is lit up by the light of God. I have been asked whether, when I am shown a soul, the light hurts my eyes. Strangely, it doesn't seem to hurt them at all.

The shape and form was that of my mother's body but was bigger. Within this beautiful bright and crystal-clear shape I could see the image of my mother's human body. But it was of a perfect young body, not the rather old and rickety body that was asleep in the chair.

It was incredibly beautiful seeing the reflection of my mother looking so young and so perfect in every way. My mother's soul turned and looked at me. I was deeply moved by what I was being shown.

I believe I was shown my mother's soul that day simply because I had asked. I had been shown my father's soul many years before, when he was dying, and I had always hoped and prayed that I would also be shown my mother's soul one day.

Your soul fills every single part of your body. There

is no part of your body that is not illuminated by this light. It's hard to explain; your soul is so tiny, but yet enormous. Your soul is a speck of God's light and is perfect and incredibly beautiful.

I am not allowed to see everyone's soul. In my life I have probably been shown several hundred souls, and I have been given glimpses of thousands of others, where the soul steps forward in the body slightly. I am always deeply moved and honoured when I am allowed to see even a glimpse of a soul. It is such a privilege.

I believe I have been shown souls so that I can share the information with others, so that I can help people to believe that they have a soul. I have been asked how I know that everyone has a soul. My answer, which may not satisfy you, is that I see a guardian angel with everyone; this guardian angel is the gatekeeper of your soul and God wouldn't have given you a guardian angel if you didn't have a soul.

My faith is very strong. I am helped, of course, by seeing angels physically all the time and sometimes seeing souls. I know that everyone has a soul, even though I can't prove it to you.

Because we have souls that are in the image of God we are more than any angel. Angels are created by God but they have no soul. We are God's children.

Angels love to be around us because we each possess a soul. When angels are with us – imperfect as we may feel we are – they are in the presence of the light of God. We embody God.

To me this is incredible. Just think about it. God loved each and every one of us so much that he has given us a part of himself. I'm not sure that we humans have really grasped just how wonderful this is.

CHAPTER THIRTEEN

Love conquers hate

IF EVERYONE COULD SEE THE BEAUTY OF THE human soul, as I do, then there would be no hate or killing or war. When I see the soul of another person, I am overwhelmed by love. This love can conquer hate if only we would let it.

In the mid-1990s, before Megan was born, people from Northern Ireland started to show up on the doorstep of the cottage in Maynooth. I never knew who sent them – I always say it was God who did.

I remember one man of about thirty-five – I will call him Paul – who sat at the kitchen table talking to me. He told me very haltingly of some of the things he had done – including planting bombs that killed people. When he was too ashamed to talk, the angels who were with him used to fill in the details – which were truly horrific. He told me that he had learned to hate Protestants very early on and that this hate was instilled in him by his uncle, who was active in the IRA. Paul's anger and hate were then fed when two cousins were killed. Paul started running messages for the IRA as a child and then moved on as a teenager to more active terrorism. He told me that it was just hitting him now what he had done, that it was as if his eyes had just been opened, and that he couldn't really understand the reason for the deep hatred he felt for Protestants. He told me that a close friend of his had died in a car crash, and that this had helped to awaken in him the futility of a life wasted – of a young person dying before his time.

Paul told me that he had only come to see me because his aunt, who had visited me previously, had insisted that he did. I remembered the aunt. She was a very thin woman, who was prematurely old from worry. She had lost sons in the Troubles and was sick with worry about who might be killed next. It was her love that sent Paul to me and he came because he knew she loved him.

Paul told me that he wanted it all to end, that he

was disgusted by the thought of how much pain and destruction he had caused. That he didn't want to be that person. He didn't want, he said, any more nightmares and any more tears. He wanted my, and the angels', help.

The angels told me to tell him he would have to work to conquer his desire to strike out in anger, to get revenge. That he should ask his guardian angel to help him to hold back, and that he had the strength to do it. I did also tell Paul, though, that it would take time, and for most of his life he would have to work hard to conquer this hate that had been instilled into him by his uncle. I told him that when he felt like striking back he should ask his guardian angel for help and remember all of the hurt and pain he felt when his own family members were killed; he should understand that others had the same feelings.

I said revenge was an unending circle and that it had to be stopped. He had to help to kill revenge, both within himself and in those around him, particularly those younger than him. I told him that peace in Northern Ireland is very important, that the angels had told me that Northern Ireland is a cornerstone for peace throughout the world – that it is supposed to serve as an example to other areas of the globe where there is violence and strife. That if Ireland can do it, then other places can do it too.

I prayed for Paul often after that and for all the people involved in the Northern Ireland conflict. I prayed that love might conquer hate.

Some years later, I met Paul again. He came up to me on Dublin's Henry Street and said, 'Remember me?' I didn't initially but when he smiled and mentioned conquering hate, I remembered. He looked different, less coiled up and stressed. Previously, he had looked as if he could lose his temper very easily. Now he looked more calm and peaceful. He told me he was still working hard to conquer his own hate, and that he was working with others in support of the Northern Ireland peace process. Talking with him that day, I realised how bright and intelligent he was and how much he might have done with his life if he hadn't had that hate instilled into him. But he was working now to make something of his life, and to make a contribution to his community.

I had my daughter Ruth with me so we only talked briefly; as he walked away I asked the angels if Paul was succeeding in conquering hate and I was told yes.

Sometimes we think that hate has only to do with big things like war or terrorism but we all have the potential to let hate into our lives, to let it poison relationships between families, friends, work colleagues and communities.

This is how what I call 'the other side' gets into our lives. Evil exists. What I call 'the devil', having grown up in a Christian tradition, really exists. And in every faith there is a name for this force of evil. I'd love to tell you he doesn't exist but he does and when we let him into our lives he will come in and exploit those weaknesses, those negative feelings within us. This happens very simply and with the smallest of things. Most of us don't even realise it is happening until we feel worked up about something or wronged in some way. It might be feeling jealous that a sibling has more money than you or that a colleague is promoted, or feeling slighted by what you perceive as an insult. Very quickly we can translate something into feeling hard done by or being a victim.

We all have the potential to take offence or want to get back at someone. We all need to learn to recognise this tendency within ourselves and to stop when we see the signs and ask our guardian angel for help. We should ask for help to stop us from striking back and instead allow love back into the relationship. I'm not talking of love as romantic love or as the love we feel for family; I'm talking about the power of love that is within all of us. It is this power of love that is so strong and visible when I am allowed to see someone's soul. If we used this power of love more our lives would be so much easier and our world a much better place.

Families can be such loving places, but it is amazing how fast hate can grow in them. A woman came to talk with me about her family. It was a big family with a big family business in which a number of brothers and sisters were involved. When things were going well and times were good the siblings were happy for one member to make the decisions and to have a bigger slice of the pie. When things started to go wrong, though, this changed completely. The company lost money because of some poor decisions and some of the brothers and sisters started to struggle financially. Tensions were running very high for a year or more. So much bitterness and hate crept into the family. They couldn't be in the same room together, let alone speak to each other.

Two members of the family came to see me – one of the sisters who was involved in the business and an aunt. They told me they were worn down by the bitterness and recriminations and wanted an end to it. Love had brought them to come to me to ask for help

An angel standing with the women told me, 'Tell them that it's very important they get the family together to sit down and talk. It should just be the brothers and sisters and their husbands and wives. No children. It's important that it's somewhere neutral, not in their offices or a home. Suggest somewhere like a hotel where they can't raise their voices. You will need to help them not to interrupt and try and get them to listen so they start to get an understanding of each other. You will need to try and make sure that no one gets up and walks away from the table.'

I told them exactly what the angel had told me. The sister protested that this was going to be hard, that she wasn't sure she could succeed. The angel answered, 'You will need to work hard to make the meeting happen but I know you will succeed because of you both getting together. You are to do your best to try and see beyond the challenges. These are bridges and you will cross over them. You need to let the others know that you love them and miss them and instil in them the confidence that if you all pull together you will all get through this.'

I told them I would pray for them and they should ask their guardian angels for help.

They had that meeting. It was just the beginning.

Two years later the family is talking. It's not always easy for them but they are all much more aware of how they nearly lost each other. They are still struggling financially and they lost an awful lot of their wealth. The family business is much smaller than it originally was but the family is still together. The last time I heard from the aunt, she told me that the family had all been together to celebrate a family christening. They were all so conscious of how, during the difficult times, such a gathering would have been impossible. While they might have less money now they were much more appreciative of the importance of having each other and of the joy that family can bring.

Often, the key to letting love conquer hate is in having the courage to take the first step.

I was sitting in Bewleys in Grafton Street in Dublin enjoying a coffee and bun. A well-dressed woman of about forty walked in. I could see two angels with her, as well as the light of her guardian angel. She stopped near me, as if noticing something, and I saw her look towards tables by the wall, where there were people sitting, and then away. I asked the angel with her without words what was the matter. 'Her heart is heavy,' was all it said.

The woman continued on walking and then stopped

at the bottom of the stairs. After a moment she turned around. The angel with her said to me, 'She has great courage. She is so afraid she will be rejected.' They didn't tell me anything more. She walked over and stopped by a table where a young woman and a young man were sitting. I could see the young girl clearly but was too far away to hear any conversation. The woman stood by the table and didn't say anything, the young woman looked up and a look of horror crossed her face. I could see an angel whispering in her ear.

I watched as the woman held out her hand in greeting. The younger woman softened and relaxed a little and gave a small smile. She didn't take her hand but stood up. The other woman drew back her outstretched hand. The angel with the woman told me they hadn't spoken for a long time, but she had felt the love she had always had for the young woman when she saw her there and had listened to the angel and overcome her fear of rejection. They stood chatting for a few minutes and I could see the love between them being rekindled. It was as if the barriers between them were melting away. As the woman walked away she turned back and the young woman looked at her and waved. I think the woman was in shock as she walked out of the café.

I asked the angel with her silently if they would be all right, if they would meet again and I was told yes, that this was just the beginning.

I'm not saying it's easy. In fact, letting love conquer hate is one of the hardest things we are asked to do in this life. We can feel so hurt and vulnerable ourselves and can feel that if we 'weaken' and don't strike back then we are giving in to another and letting ourselves down. The person who allows love to conquer hate is not weak. He or she is very strong and is a beacon of hope for all of us.

It is easy to let the other side in and to strike back. It is much harder to stop and resist seeking revenge. We need to start by doing it in small things, holding back the hurtful remark, not repeating gossip, not taking pleasure in another's misfortune. In learning to hold back on the little things we get stronger and this will make us much more able to resist actions that will lead to hate and hurt.

Ask your guardian angel to help you. It will whisper in your ear and remind you not to strike back when you are tempted. It still won't be easy. You might have to bite your tongue. I know that I find it hard and my guardian angel has to keep reminding me. You are much stronger than you might think – the power of the love that is within you is enormous.

When you don't listen to your guardian angel you will feel guilt. Your guardian angel wants you to be happy and it knows you will be happier within yourself if you learn to conquer hate, so it will do everything possible to teach you. Your guardian angel will keep nagging at you not to give in to hate and will help you to learn new and kinder ways of being. This is a continuous process and love is called upon to conquer hate time and time again – sometimes between the same people.

I know a family with lots of children and two of the boys are constantly at loggerheads with each other. These teenagers left school early and have no work because of the difficult economic situation. They are living at home and feeling inadequate and useless. They are constantly running each other down in the nastiest way and rows frequently break out between them. Sometimes the rows are verbal and sometimes they beat each other up.

Last week, they had a terrible row and one of the boys ran away. His mother and sisters went looking for him. They were desperately worried about where he might be and about what he might do, in his pain and desperation, to himself or others. They were so concerned that they got the local police involved. At four o'clock in the morning, after many hours of searching frantically, they found him and brought him home.

His brother was so relieved to see him. He had been terrified of what might happen as a result of their row, terrified that he might actually lose his brother. They made their peace. Love conquered hate – for a while.

I know these boys will fight again but I pray that the example of the love their sisters and mother showed them in searching for him for so long will help to grow the love that is between all of them. All I can do is keep praying that the boys will find work and will lose some of their frustrations. I know they are good boys and the angels tell me that they are both trying not to let the hate in, not to give in to the frustration that they are feeling.

The person who allows love to conquer hate is not weak. He or she is very strong and is a beacon of hope for all of us.

Angels help to ensure that where possible love conquers hate. They provide opportunities but lots of the time we pass them by. The woman I told you about in Bewleys Café seized the chance she was offered.

The angels need our help at times, though. We are all sometimes called upon to be peacemakers and it is important that we take these opportunities, remembering that we are called upon to make peace, not to take sides. This is not an easy job. It's not easy to stay detached and loving when you are standing between two sides that are full of anger and hate for each other.

I remember, many years ago, watching the angels and a peacemaker at work. Joe and I were with the children, who were still very young, on Dublin's Meath Street. It's a busy street with market stalls selling fruit and vegetables and all kinds of things. We had just come out of the old department store, Frawley's, and were standing looking at the window display when the shouting and roaring began. There were two women, one of them a street seller, just up the way roaring at each other. I was quite shocked at the language they were using in front of children and it looked as if they might even come to blows. Everyone stopped to look. I could see angels surrounding them and going between them, trying to keep the peace. From nowhere, a third woman appeared; she seemed to know the two women and stood in between them.

They kept swearing and cursing but over time they quietened down. I have no idea what the woman said but she was a peacemaker brought in by the angels to help. Angels encircled them all. A few minutes later, the woman left with one of the women who was fighting. Love had again overcome hate, this time thanks to the intervention of a peacemaker.

CHAPTER FOURTEEN

Angels dry our tears

A FEW YEARS AGO, I WAS VISITING A FRIEND IN hospital. I went to the bathroom and, as I walked back into the ward, my guardian angel told me to look at the bed on my right. There was an elderly man asleep in the bed. His guardian angel had opened up and he was tenderly holding on to the elderly man's soul. The guardian angel, who gave a male appearance, was standing at the head of the bed and his hands seemed to be reaching ever so slightly into the elderly man's body and lifting the man's soul a little out of his body. The elderly man's soul was glowing brightly. The guardian angel told me without words that he only had a short time to live. Standing by the bed, looking at the elderly man with a look of such sadness on his face, was a young man of about twenty-five. I believe it was his grandson.

I sat down by my friend's bed, which was across the room. I glanced over at the young man as often as I could without drawing attention to myself and I prayed for help for him. He just stood there, never moving. On one occasion when I glanced across, the light of the young man's guardian angel opened up. The guardian angel was enormous but didn't give an appearance of being male or female. The angel's robes were a very light gold and green colour. The angel embraced the young man with such tenderness and love, trying to console him in his grief.

At one point, I walked to the water cooler to get a glass of water for my friend. The young man still stood there, unmoving, looking at his grandfather asleep in the bed. I could see the elderly man's guardian angel was still holding on to his soul. As I walked past, I saw the young man's guardian angel raise its right hand in front of his heart. A light started to radiate from the angel's hand to the man's chest. As the angel rotated its hand slowly it turned its head and spoke to me without words. 'Lorna, I am putting some light into the emptiness that this young man is feeling in his heart. I am trying to help with the grieving for his grandfather.'

There were two other angels on either side of the young man and they were holding on to him and looking down at him. They were tall and elegant and gave a female appearance. These angels were dressed in a watery-blue colour with a touch of silver and I could faintly see the movement of wings. I thanked his guardian angel for allowing the other angels to be around the man, to help him in his time of need. I never saw the young man leave – all I know is that later on, when I looked up, he was gone.

When you are with someone you love and you know that their time is short, look at them a bit more closely and be confident in knowing that their guardian angel is holding on to them, taking care of them, and will bring them safely home to Heaven.

Grieving is something that few of us will escape. It's a part of love and it really hurts. Our guardian angels try and make it easier for us.

I loved my mother-in-law very much. This may sound strange, but I never called her by a name – her name was Liz, but I never recall calling her anything to her face. I used to refer to her as Joe's mum. We used to see her once a month or so and the children (she died before Megan was born) loved her.

I was in the kitchen preparing dinner on my own one evening when the Angel Hosus tapped on the kitchen door. We sat down at the table to talk. 'Lorna, you are going to start to grieve,' Hosus said.

I looked at him in shock, saying, 'Who for?'

He quietly replied, 'Joe's mother.'

'But she's doing OK,' I protested in shock.

Hosus looked at me with love. 'God will be taking her soon, Lorna.' I felt so sad as Angel Hosus said these words. He reached out and took my hand. 'Don't be sad, Lorna. You know it's only her body that dies. Her soul lives, and she will be going back home to Heaven, and you will see her again one day. You are going to start to grieve for her as soon as I leave, Lorna.'

When Hosus left, I sat at the table and I cried and cried. She had been such a caring and loving woman and had always accepted me in a way many other people didn't. She was so supportive when Joe and I got engaged and really welcomed me into her family.

I never told anyone how upset I was though – not Joe, not anyone. I cried a lot, but never in front of anyone. I told no one I was grieving. How could I tell anyone what Hosus had told me? Each time I was with her, I smiled and showed her all the love I could, but deep down I was wondering whether this was the last time I would see her.

I knew there was something more to this grieving. I loved my mother-in-law, but she was elderly and wasn't a major part of my life. I didn't see her every week so I couldn't understand why I was feeling the pain of grief so strongly, and why I was feeling it before she was even sick. I would learn later from the angels why this was happening.

Joe's mother's health deteriorated as Hosus had told me it would and about a month after I had started the grieving process she was admitted to hospital. She was there about six weeks before she died. On one of her first days in hospital I arrived with Joe to visit her. As I walked into the ward, I could see her guardian angel right behind her, taking hold of her soul, lifting it gently forward with great love. It was only fractionally forward in her body, but I could see the magnificent light of her soul. Her guardian angel's wings were partially open and curved protectively around her. Each time I visited after this, her guardian angel had lifted her soul further forward out of her body.

On her last day, she was moved into a different ward. As I walked in, I could see that her soul was completely out of her body with her guardian angel behind her, holding it. When someone is dying, their guardian angel does not let go of their soul for an instant. Whenever I see a guardian angel who is about to accompany a soul to Heaven, the physical appearance of the angel changes. Joe's mum's guardian angel gave less of a human appearance and appeared to be less solid, less dense. It was as if it had taken its clothes off in order to leave them here on earth, in order to be purer for going to Heaven. While its human features were less distinctive, I could see and feel the compassion and love that the angel had for Joe's mother as it was preparing to bring her soul back home.

This is one of the most joyous times for any guardian angel – bringing a soul safely back to Heaven – and I could feel an incredible joy radiating from Joe's mother's guardian angel.

Joe's mum's guardian angel was so beautiful – but her soul was much, much more beautiful. There was such a light radiating from it, and I was allowed for a moment to see a human appearance within the soul. She was facing her guardian angel and then turned around and looked directly at me. She looked much younger than she had been when I first met her. She was like she would have been as a twenty-year-old, but much more radiant

Her breathing had become very laboured but her guardian angel told me she was past all pain. I sat there by her bedside, holding her hand, with Joe and Joe's uncle beside me. I had no idea how long it would be until she went to Heaven, but I knew it wouldn't be long. After about an hour, I leant over her and whispered in her ear that I loved her. As I said this, I heard her soul communicating to me without words. She told me to take Joe away so that he wouldn't be there when she died. I did as she asked and suggested to Joe that we go and have something to eat, leaving his uncle by the hospital bed.

We came back an hour or so later. As we walked through the hospital towards her ward the place was thronged with angels and I knew she had gone to Heaven.

Joe was devastated by his mother's death. He loved her a lot. His da had died when he was only fourteen, so for much of life he had only had his mother. After Joe's mother died I found I wasn't grieving nearly as hard as I had beforehand. I wondered about this.

Months later, Angel Hosus explained this to me a little. He told me that they were helping me to grieve so that the grieving for Joe would be a little less intense. I did, of course, know that Joe would die young: Angel Elijah had told me so all those years ago. And he did suffer constantly from ill health, but I had no idea of when he would be called to Heaven. Angel Hosus told me that God and the angels were helping to prepare me by allowing me to feel intense and deep grief and know at the same time that I would survive. This gave me the courage and confidence to know that I would eventually get through it.

When Joe died, some years later, the grief I felt was overwhelming. As I say, the angels had told me that the grief with Joe's mum's death had been partly to prepare me but, to be honest, I am not sure anyone can be prepared for the death of a loved one. They had also told me that the grieving for my mother-in-law lessened the grief I felt after Joe's death. But to be honest my grief felt so devastating that I have no idea how it could have been more.

I did get through it, though. The angels never allowed me to give up. They gave me the strength to help me, in time, to move on. But it did take time and it was very painful. For years after Joe's death I would feel tremendous pain, particularly around family events like birthdays or confirmations. Now, more than ten years on, I don't grieve any more but I do miss him.

As I have been writing this, I have asked why I felt

the grief before Joe's mum died, rather than afterwards, and why I needed to feel it so intensely some six years before Joe died. The angels haven't given me an answer, though.

We grieve for the loss of someone we love because they are not with us here physically. In our pain and despair, we need to hold on to the certainty that our loved one had a soul that lives forever and has gone to Heaven, and that we will meet them again some day. Angels help us to get through our grief, to continue to live our lives even after the loss of someone who was very precious to us.

Long before I started to write, a woman called Maura – who used to come and see me – told me a lovely story of how the angels had comforted her one Christmas after her husband had died. Christmas can be a sad time for people who have lost someone they love. This Christmas, Maura was at her kitchen sink, washing dishes and remembering the good times when her husband and her children were all together – the birthdays, christenings, but particularly the Christmases. Her children were all grown up now, but were still very close to her. She had a wonderful family but that didn't fill the loneliness of missing the man she had loved dearly. She was feeling so sad and so alone and there were tears in her eyes as she begged,

'Just give me a sign. Show me that you really are there, that you haven't gone away completely.'

She followed some instinct and just left the dishes in the sink and walked across the kitchen and out into the garden. The weather was cold and changeable and she stood there in the cold looking around her, wondering to herself whether her husband could really be in Heaven, whether he could still be with her in spirit. She looked at trees and plants that had grown since he had died and then, out of nowhere it seemed to her, it started to snow.

Maura laughed and, feeling her husband's presence in some way, she spoke to him aloud. 'So you have me out in the garden, and now it's starting to snow, I'm freezing and it's snowing.' The snowflakes kept falling and then, for no reason she could explain, one falling snowflake attracted her. It was no different from any of the other snowflakes that were falling around her but she had a very strong urge to catch that particular snowflake. She reached out and the snowflake landed on her hand. She looked at it in amazement. The snowflake wasn't melting. As she looked more closely she realised that it wasn't a snow-flake. It was a feather, a tiny feather no bigger than a snowflake. There were no birds around. There was nowhere it could have come from. As she touched the feather, tears came into her eyes and she said a heartfelt thank-you. She thanked God and the angels and she thanked her much-loved husband.

> **We need to hold on to the certainty that our loved one had a soul that lives forever and has gone to Heaven, and that we will meet them again some day.**

Receiving this little feather filled Maura's heart with joy. She knew it was a sign that her husband was happy in Heaven, but that he was still with her whenever she needed him. It gave her the hope and strength to face the future, to know that she wasn't alone. Maura always had faith, but this feather rekindled her faith and her belief that her husband's soul was in Heaven. That she would see him again one day. She held that little feather tightly in her hand as she walked back into the house to look for something small and special to put her precious feather in, so that she could keep it safe and look at it, and know that her husband was there with her in spirit and that God and His angels were there with her also.

I see angels surrounding and comforting people who are feeling grief. But, often, we are so griefstricken and desolate that we don't feel this consolation. Try and remind yourself that these angels are there with you. Angels will give us signs of encouragement, particularly at this time, and often they work through others who come to console us or to offer words of support.

Maura was given this sign from God and the angels to help give her the courage to go on. To rekindle her belief that her husband's soul live forever, a belief that had nearly been extinguished by the pain of her grief.

CHAPTER FIFTEEN

I have been shown wonderful things . . .

THE ANGEL MICHAEL HAS SHOWN ME A FUTURE where everyone sees angels physically, as I do. Where everyone can talk with them, as I do. Where our guardian angels are our best friends and we listen and follow their advice.

I have always said that I don't know why I have been allowed to see angels physically and you or others haven't. I am an ordinary person and I have always believed that if I can see angels then everyone else can. As I talk more about what I see, I am starting to understand that one of the reasons I have been allowed to see angels is to help to share with you what our future could be like, to help you to understand how our lives could be if we could all see and talk with angels.

I have no idea how long it will take for us to evolve so that everyone will be able to see and talk with angels, when this will happen or how many genera- tions it will take. I am very encouraged, though, by the signs I am being shown of people – particularly young people – becoming more aware and I know that the pace of this development is speeding up. I know it will be an evolutionary process, that some people will become more aware first and will be able to see angels while others still can't. If we as humans make the right decisions we will all eventually be able to see our guardian angels physically.

Many young people, while they are not seeing angels physically as I do, seem to me to be responding much more to what their guardian angel is telling them. This is not just because young people have always been more open than adults. I know the young people of today are more open than my generation were – I see it in their behaviour every day.

Yesterday, I was standing outside the supermarket and a group of teenagers walked past. The light of the guardian angel with one of the girls opened up briefly, showing me a female appearance. It stooped over the young girl it was guiding and seemed to have its two hands on her shoulder. It whispered briefly to the girl and then the light of the guardian angel closed. Instantly, the girl went over and took a bag from one of the other teenagers. The angels with her confirmed that the guardian angel had asked her to help her friend, and she had heard and responded instantly. I know it's a very simple example, but when you listen to angels all the time it is in fact very simple.

Recently, I was walking through a park that was full of flowers and shrubs with big blossoms. As I walked along one of the paths, an angel whispered to me to look ahead. There were a lot of people around. The angel whispered to me again, telling me to look at a young boy of about eight. I watched with fascination as the boy played with the energy of the blossom of the flower. He was touching the energy from the blossom and sticking his fingers into it and stirring it around with his finger. He laughed, feeling the tingling sensation of the energy on his finger. I could see that he was spellbound but had no idea what he was seeing.

He was seeing the energy that I have seen around all living things since I was a baby.

We all have the potential to become more spiritually

aware and more open. This potential is a gift that God has given us, but many people become fearful. It takes courage to acknowledge that God exists, that you have a soul and a guardian angel who is the gatekeeper of that soul.

I know from personal experience that it takes courage. Until my mid-fifties I was very reluctant to talk about what I see and hear, and hardly talked about it at all. I was afraid I would be ridiculed and laughed at, that people would say I was crazy.

I always say that I didn't choose the time to start talking about what I see but that God did. God chose this time because He wants us to speed up our spiritual evolution and He chose this time of change and challenge in the world.

A lot of different things help to open us up spiritually, to become more spiritually aware. I have talked about many of them in this book. Prayer does it. So does becoming more aware of God's presence, acknowledging that we are more than just flesh and blood – that we have a soul as well. Believing in angels, and asking for their help, makes us more receptive or sensitive to God's message and helps us to get closer to God. So does becoming more conscious and appreciative of the ordinary things of life, spending more time in nature, silence or meditation.

In getting closer to God we open up spiritually. God wants and helps us to become more spiritually aware. This is a part of his plan for the evolution of humanity.

As we become more spiritually aware we become more compassionate, more given to seeing the good in others, and this make us gentler and kinder. What some people call 'intuition' becomes stronger as people listen more to God and the angels and learn to respond to what they are told. We start to see more energy around people and living things, and to see more of the beauty in life.

As we become more spiritually aware we become better and more fulfilled people.

I pray every day and ask that people all over the world, of all religions, will grow more spiritually aware and be less afraid.

A few years ago, an eleven-year-old called Suzy asked me about the energy she was seeing. I was able to help her to understand more of what she was seeing and what to look out for in the future. I met her again recently and there were three angels around her. I had to smile as one of the angels was dressed in the same style of clothes that teenage boys wear – although the colour scheme was rather different: silvers and greys and navy. I talked with Suzy as the angel who was dressed like a teenage boy kept saying, 'She has something more to tell you. You'll have to have patience.'

We had been talking for about ten minutes when Suzy finally said what was on her mind. 'I let God and the angels down,' she said. The angels with her shook their heads.

Suzy explained that she had been out with two of her friends and they had talked about the strange mist that was coming from the hedging. They were talking about how weird it was.

Suzy wanted to explain that they were seeing energy and that she could see energy too, but she was afraid they would laugh at her. She was very disappointed at herself for not having the courage to explain to them what they were seeing.

I smiled at her. 'You didn't let God and the angels down. Your friends will see it again and you will have another opportunity to explain it to them.' I know that the next time this happens she will have the courage to talk to her friends about what she sees.

Fear is one of the things that stops us from evolving spiritually. Other things that stop us doing so include placing too much emphasis on material things, and acting as if money and 'things' are all there is to life. Getting caught up in day-to-day activities – doing too much and believing we have no time – is another way.

If we don't allow peace and quiet into our lives, at least occasionally, it is very hard to hear God and his angels.

Listening to the other side – even in small petty things, like making a nasty remark or being selfish – hinders your spiritual development. Satan, or whatever you call the other side in your religion, certainly doesn't want us to evolve spiritually, and we strengthen his hand when we listen to him rather than to God or the angels.

Everyone needs to play their part. We all have a part to play in the spiritual evolution of humanity. Everyone must help and encourage others to play their part as well. This is why praying for our leaders is so important, and something we must all be aware of.

Sitting at the kitchen table, wondering what to write in this final chapter, the Angel Michael took my hand and showed me a vision. I was on a hill overlooking a wide area of countryside. Below me there were thousands of people – men, women and children of all ages – in a big circle. From their appearance and clothes I could tell they were of different nationalities and different religions. The place was full of angels and watching them it was clear to me that the people could see and talk with the angels that were there with them. In addition to guardian angels and other angels there many angels of prayer streaming up into the sky to Heaven.

The people were at prayer. They were praying aloud and it was as if different languages were being used but yet it was all part of one big prayer. I could hear the hum of their prayer. In the centre, surrounded by angels, was the person who was leading the prayer. I couldn't tell whether it was a man or woman. However, it wasn't as if this person was more important than the others; they were just leading the prayer.

People were praying in whatever position felt most comfortable to them, standing, sitting on the ground or lying down, and everyone seemed to me to be praying with their heart and soul. They were all fully engrossed in their prayer, and enjoying it.

The place felt so peaceful and looked so bright – almost as if a light was shining from the earth underneath them. The people looked bright – brighter than anyone I have ever seen before. Everyone looked perfect, full of life and vibrancy, even the very elderly, and no one there seemed disabled or sick in any way. From my high vantage point I could see a circle of light around the huge gathering of people. Outside this circle, I could see rolling green hills and trees.

Again, everything looked so much more alive and vibrant than it does in our world today.

The vision faded and I found myself back at my kitchen table with Angel Michael.

'I would have loved to stay there. Can I not go back?' I asked Angel Michael. He smiled and shook his head. I continued, 'That was like a little glimpse of Heaven – but I know it was the earth, not Heaven.'

Angel Michael replied, 'That is humanity's future, if it chooses it. If it makes the right decisions and grows spiritually.'

 We all have a part to play in the spiritual evolution of humanity.

The Angel Hope appeared briefly beside me, filling me with hope for this wonderful future for humanity and giving me the courage and strength to know that we *can* make the right decisions to build this amazing world.

Prayers from *A Message of Hope from the Angels* by Lorna Byrne

These are all prayers that God gave His angels to give me. God has given me permission to share them with you and your loved ones.

A Prayer of Thanks

Thank you for all the blessings you have
    bestowed upon me, my God.
The blessing of having a soul, that speck of
    your light;
The blessing of the gift of my guardian
    angel for eternity, that never leaves me
    even for one second;
The blessing of the peace and love that
    dwells in me;
The blessing of the family you have given me;
The blessing of those you send into my life
    for companionship;
The blessing of living in harmony with
    those around me;
The blessing of my labour, my work;
The blessings of all the material things I
    have in my life, big and small;
The blessings of this wonderful world and
    the nature around me.
Thank you, my God, for all the things I
    forget to thank you for.
And most of all, thank you, my God, for
    continuing to bless my life.
Amen.

Prayer of Thy Healing Angels
That is carried from God by Michael,
Thy Archangel

Pour out, Thy Healing Angels,
Thy Heavenly Host upon me,
And upon those that I love,
Let me feel the beam of Thy
Healing Angels upon me,
The light of Your Healing Hands.
I will let Thy Healing begin,
Whatever way God grants it,
Amen.

A Prayer for Joy in My Life

Please God,
Take this cloud of darkness away.
Shine your light upon me.
Send your angels to help me.
Give me the courage and strength
To start to feel the joy in my life again.
Amen.

A Prayer for Hard Times

God,

Pour the grace of hope upon me and allow
me always to see the light of hope
burning brightly in front of me.

Light up the darkness by filling me with
faith and hope and allowing me to receive
the comfort of your love.

Give me the courage and strength to know
that I will get through these hard times.

Fill me with the joy and trust of knowing
that I am your child and that you will
care for me and those I love.

Hear my prayer.

Amen.

Prayer for Forgiveness and Peace of Mind

God,
Please forgive me for all my imperfections.
For all the wrong I have done.
Give me the grace to forgive those that have
    hurt me.
Amen.

Prayer for Forgiveness for Those
Who Have Hurt Me

Dear God,
Please forgive those that have hurt me
    because I forgive them.
Amen.

Lorna's writing has touched so many people across the world. Here, just a few share their thoughts on the books.

'Through Lorna's books, and open-mindedness, you feel like you've just met your best friend whom you've known all your life. She has the gift of connecting with all her readers, and for those lucky to be in her presence, this connection is magnified tenfold.' Martha

'An angel herself, Lorna's words have not only enlightened my life but enriched it as well. I feel loved more then ever by my Angels and know I am never alone. This book will change your life!' Cristina, New York City

'Inspirational, exhilarating and moving.' Órla

'This book changed the way I think. I am open to angels now and talk to them all the time, I also passed these books to my family and friends who loved them just as much. Lorna you're my hero.' Irene, Omagh

'Thank you, Lorna, for your beautiful story.' Kim, Wisconsin

'Lorna's understanding of who God is, as revealed through her experiences with angels, is the God I always hoped He would be. Bigger than one religion, more forgiving, with a sense of humour and immeasurable love. *Stairways to Heaven* is a source of comfort and hope.' Claire

'Your books have been inspirational at a time of great difficulty. You have made me realise I should listen to my angels and that I'm not on my own.' Louise, Stratford-upon-Avon

'*Stairways to Heaven* made me feel me a beautiful connection to you, to my angel, to love itself and more importantly, to hope. I really feel inspired by your message.' Janny, Mexico

'Nothing will ever give you more comfort than reading this book.' Mary, Kilmarnock

'Before reading your books my thought was that angels were true but too far away from me, now I talk everyday with them and I feel that they never leave me.' Gisella, Italy

'Thank you for your courage to share your life.' Ela, Poland

'The impact that *Angels in my Hair* has had on my life is simple – I don't worry any more. Life is very uncertain for me at the moment, but I'm just going with the flow, doing what I can, but knowing that I am being looked after and that all will be well in the end. Such peace of mind is priceless, thank you.' Jenny, Powys

'Being a young person (18) I find not many people my age know about what there is out there and how much help there is on offer to us all. I tell my friends everything I know, and even if they don't believe me, I know they are still listening and absorbing that information, which hopefully has some kind of positive impact. Lorna Byrne has given me that extra knowledge and comfort that I can now share around.' Zeria, London

'Lorna, your books helped restore my faith. You have given me comfort knowing that my dad was not alone when he passed away. I can't begin to explain how much you have helped me. Thank you so much for writing these books.' Orla, Derry.

'Through your book you helped me to have more faith, to be a more spiritual person, to be more patient. I'm sure I found you because my guardian angel guided me to you and wanted me to learn from you that he is with me always.' Adriana, Costa Rica

'Thank you and the angels with all my heart and soul Lorna. When I think of my guardian angel which is more and more often these days, I feel like my heart smiles.' Mary

'These books will open your eyes if your heart is willing.' Andria

To find out more about Lorna Byrne go to www.lornabyrne.com

Here you can:

Add your wishes and prayers to Lorna's prayer scroll.

'Years ago the angels handed me a prayer scroll and told me that when I was praying I should hold it in my hand and that the angels would join me in praying for everything contained within it.

When I'm in a meditative state of prayer I hold in my hand this spiritual scroll with every name and every request written on it and I hand this scroll to God.

I invite you to send me your thoughts, joys and worries so that they can be included.

I won't be able to reply individually to your notes but be assured I will make sure they are included in the prayer scroll and in my and the angels' prayers. There is naturally no charge and everything is treated with confidence.'

LORNA

Sign up to receive Lorna's quarterly email newsletter.

Read more of the wisdom that Lorna has been given by the angels.

See where Lorna is speaking and doing signings.

Watch videos and read interviews with Lorna.

ALSO BY LORNA BYRNE

Stairways to Heaven

The overwhelming response of readers to Lorna Byrne – regardless of religious beliefs – is that she gives them back hope, helping them to realise that no matter how alone they might feel they have a guardian angel by their side.

Lorna Byrne sees and talks with angels every day and has done since she was a baby. She sees them as clearly as the rest of us see rocks and stones and trees. In *Stairways to Heaven* Lorna tells true-life stories about the ways that angels help us. She describes how they helped her pull her own life together after her husband died and how she has seen them help other people.

Stairways to Heaven includes never before revealed secrets of your guardian angel, including how your guardian angel was chosen, how you are the only person this angel will ever come to earth with, and how you know your guardian angel's name . . . even if you have forgotten it.

'Gives hope and a sense of peace, something that the Church, in many instances, has been unable to do.'

The Times

CORONET

10% of the author's royalties from the sale of *Stairways to Heaven* are being donated to charity. For details of the charities benefiting please see www.lornabyrne.com

ALSO BY LORNA BYRNE

Angels in my Hair

Angels in my Hair is the autobiography of a modern-day mystic, an Irish woman with powers of the saints of old.

When she was a child, people thought Lorna was 'retarded' because she did not seem to be focusing on the world around her. Instead, Lorna was seeing angels and spirits.

As Lorna tells the story of her life, the reader meets, as she did, the creatures from the spirit worlds who also inhabit our own – mostly angels of an astonishing beauty and variety – including the prophet Elijah and an Archangel – but also the spirits of people who have died.

This remarkable book is the testimony of a woman who sees things beyond the range of our everyday experience.

'Those who see angels are close to being angels. In this book, Lorna beautifully and graphically describes angels and how they work.'
William Roache, MBE, author of *Soul on the Street*

'The world has discovered a modest mystic that it might do well to listen to.'   *Daily Mail*

'*Angels in my Hair* is a very simply and softly written narra-tive, one that managed to grip me emotionally (tears were shed) and made me reflect.'

Sunday Independent

arrow books